SHE RISES

Insights and Wisdom from the Women of The Masterful Coach Collective®

Presented by Molly Claire

Michelle Keil	Carla Green	Margo Fordonski
Jackie Swainson	Kelly Arthur	Eugenie D. Basu
Sondra Sperry	Marianne Brereton	Angela Gaskin
Maria Hendershot	Midore Takada	Patti Britt Kohler

Publishing support provided by
Ignite Press
55 Shaw Ave. Suite 204
Clovis, CA 93612
www.IgnitePress.us

ISBN: 979-8-9997301-0-7
ISBN: 979-8-9997301-1-4 (E-book)

For bulk purchases and for booking, contact:

Molly Claire
team@mollyclaire.com

Library of Congress Control Number: 2025917482

Cover design by Usman Tariq
Edited by Elizabeth Arterberry
Interior design by Jetlaunch

FIRST EDITION

The Authors

Molly Claire

Master Coach Mentor, Elite Coach for Women Ready to Rise

🌐 www.mollyclaire.com

🎙 The Life, Mastered Podcast: www.mollyclaire.com/blog

📷 instagram.com/mollyclairecoaching

in linkedin.com/in/molly-claire-coaching

Michelle Keil

"The Doodle Coach," Master Certified Holistic Coach, Doodling Instructor and Coach

🌐 thedoodlecoach.com

📷 instagram.com/michellekeilcoaching

f facebook.com/michellekeilcoaching

in linkedin.com/in/michelle-keil-350440221

Carla Green
Master Life Coach

instagram.com/carlagreen.coaching

facebook.com/CarlaGreenCoaching

Margo Fordonski
Master Certified Holistic Life Coach and Grief Educator

Margofordonski.com

linkedin.com/in/margo-fordonski-033b27a6

instagram.com/margofordonski_lifecoach

facebook.com/margofordonskilifecoach

Jackie Swainson

Master Certified Life Coach, Speaker,
Workshop Presenter, Board Governance Advisor

jackieswainsoncoach.com

mollyclaire.com/directory-of-life-coaches

instagram.com/jackieswainsoncoach

facebook.com/Jackieswainsoncoach

Kelly Arthur

Certified Life Coach & Licensed Therapist

kellyarthurcoaching.com

instagram.com/kelly_arthur_coaching

linkedin.com/in/kellyarthur-9b9b645

Eugenie D. Basu
Master Certified Life Coach

🌐 askeugenie.com

Sondra Sperry
Holistic Master Certified Coach

🌐 coachwithsondra.com

f facebook.com/sondra.sperry

📷 instagram.com/sondrasperry

Marianne Brereton
*Clinical EFT Practitioner
and Breathwork Facilitator*

🌐 mbeftandbreathwork.com

📷 instagram.com/mariannebreretoncoaching

f facebook.com/marianne.brereton.2025

in linkedin.com/in/marianne-brereton

Angela Gaskin
Master Coach

🌐 angelagaskincoaching.com

f facebook.com/profile.php?id=61561552352875

Maria Hendershot
Master Coach

🌐 joyfulreinvention.com

📷 instagram.com/mariahendershot.coaching

Midore Takada
*Master Certified Coach | Holistic &
Trauma-Informed Life Coach | Advanced
Certification in Motherhood & Family Life
Coaching*

🌐 midoretakada.com

📷 instagram.com/midore_takada_coaching

f facebook.com/midore.takada

Patti Britt Kohler

Master Life & Relationship Coach, Speaker, Entrepreneur

🌐 pattibrittcoaching.com

📷 instagram.com/pattibrittcoaching

in linkedin.com/in/pattibrittkohler

Table of Contents

INTRODUCTION 1

CHAPTER 1: Wholeness over Hustle: The New Standard
for High-Level Women in Business 3
    BY MOLLY CLAIRE

CHAPTER 2: Discover Your True Self Through Doodles:
Because Pens and Markers Are Cheaper than Therapy. 17
    BY MICHELLE KEIL

CHAPTER 3: The Message in the Feeling 31
    BY CARLA GREEN

CHAPTER 4: Grieving and Growing: How to Rebuild Life
After the Unthinkable 41
    BY MARGO FORDONSKI

CHAPTER 5: Mirror, Mirror on the Wall. . . What the Heck
Happened?: Stepping into Your Worth as a Woman of a
"Certain Age" 55
    BY JACKIE SWAINSON

CHAPTER 6: Self-Care Reimagined: The Radical Act of
Choosing Yourself in a World That Taught You Not To 69
    BY KELLY ARTHUR

CHAPTER 7: Inner Boundaries:
The Secret to Feeling Happy, Joyous, and Free. 83
  BY EUGENIE D. BASU

CHAPTER 8: When the Soul Whispers "Enough":
Heeding the Quiet Voice That Calls for Rest, Not Perfection . . . 95
  BY SONDRA SPERRY

CHAPTER 9: What the Brain Needs to Heal, and the
Body Longs to Feel: Restore Regulation and Joy
with EFT Tapping and Breathwork 109
  BY MARIANNE BRERETON

CHAPTER 10: Perfectly Disguised:
Behind The Mask Of Having It All Together 121
  BY ANGELA GASKIN

CHAPTER 11: Joyful Reinvention:
The Joy of Coming Home to Yourself 135
  BY MARIA HENDERSHOT

CHAPTER 12: From Burnout to Purpose:
Redefining Success from the Inside Out. 149
  BY MIDORE TAKADA

CHAPTER 13: Why I Make Grown Men Cry 163
  BY PATTI BRITT KOHLER

CONCLUSION 177

**ARE YOU INTERESTED IN BECOMING A MASTER
CERTIFIED COACH?** 179

WILL YOU SHARE THE LOVE? 181

Introduction

I 'm so glad you're here, *and I'm about to tell you why.*

I'm writing this introduction to you from my bedroom closet, sitting on the floor with my laptop. It's the same spot I sat in about a decade ago when I made a bold decision to hire a coach and change my life.

I was facing divorce, stepping into becoming a single mom of three, trying to heal from chronic fatigue, starting my business, and managing about a million and one fears and doubts. With a deep pit of fear in my stomach and tears streaming down my face, I decided to say "yes."

I had already trained as a life coach. I'd invested time, energy, and money into being able to help others; I was doing it every day. I knew the power of coaching.

Yet, in that moment, when life, finances, my health, and my future felt so uncertain, it seemed like a crazy time to make such a significant financial investment.

As I sat there in the closet, tears flowing, I was also facing one of my worst nightmares: the potential of reliving my mom's life. She had been chronically burnt out, exhausted, barely making ends meet as a single mom, and she had been riddled with guilt for not being able to be there for me and my siblings.

I didn't want that life. I wouldn't give that life to my kids. And I knew that my mom, may she rest in peace, did not want that for me.

Thankfully, I knew an important truth.

As a coach, *I understood that my own beliefs were the key to making a different life possible. I knew that I wasn't stuck in any moment, or any circumstance. And I could feel in my bones that I had the opportunity to create a different life, my ideal life, the life that would be amazing for me, my kids, and my future self, too.*

And so, I said, "yes." I clicked the button on my laptop and hired the best coach I knew. It was the first of many moments that I would say "yes" to myself and choose to better my well-being and quality of life, knowing they were worth fighting for.

I don't know why you picked up this book, but it's no accident that you did. Within these pages, you'll find wisdom from some of the most compassionate and masterful coaches on the planet.

Together, we are here to show you what is possible for you. We're here to teach you about the power of your mind, the importance of your own emotions, and the potential you possess to bring your greatest desires to fruition.

I don't know what struggles you're facing or will yet face. I don't know what from your past still follows you, or what worries you may hold about your future. And while I don't know much about the details of your life, I do know an absolute truth about you: you are more powerful than you can begin to realize.

The words in this book are for you. We are here to remind you of a few things that a part of you already knows. You matter. Your feelings matter. Your desires matter. Your brain is powerful. Your heart is wise. Believe it or not, what you want in life gets to be the center of your universe. The future is truly yours.

This book is for you. . . Now, let's get started.

CHAPTER 1

Wholeness over Hustle: The New Standard for High-Level Women in Business

Molly Claire

Master Coach Mentor, Elite Coach for Women Ready to Rise

www.mollyclaire.com

The Life, Mastered Podcast: www.mollyclaire.com/blog

instagram.com/mollyclairecoaching

linkedin.com/in/molly-claire-coaching

Molly Claire is a master coach and high-level mentor for driven, purpose-centered women who are ready to rise to their next chapter in business and life. A best-selling author, national speaker, and top 3% podcaster, Molly brings over a decade of expertise in helping entrepreneurs and coaches build six- and seven-figure businesses with purpose, precision, and self-trust.

As the founder of The Masterful Coach Collective, she trains coaches and leaders to master the four fundamentals of lasting change: mindset, emotion, nervous system, and aligned action. Her signature high-touch mentorship supports high-responsibility women navigating greater business success, visibility, and expansion with depth and authenticity.

Molly's clients often say she sees them more clearly than they see themselves and helps them lead with more ease, clarity, and confidence than ever before. She feels deeply grateful each day that she is surrounded by strong women doing meaningful work. Molly is the proud mom of three children and a sweet rescue pup that's always at her feet.

• • •

If you're a high-achieving, high-responsibility woman who is done running on empty and ready to feel deeply alive, whole, and fulfilled—this chapter is for you.

You'll soon learn that your next level of success, impact, and income won't come from pushing harder, but from holding still long enough to allow your brilliance to shine.

Whether you're single or have a partner, you feel like the "glue" holding everything together. You carry the mental and emotional weight that no one sees, *but you certainly feel* it. Your list of responsibilities is overwhelming (and never-ending). You can't seem to say "no" nearly often enough and you find yourself *worn out, spread thin, and wondering where the fulfillment is that you're desperately craving.*

This is your invitation to reclaim yourself and step into an entirely new way of being—one rooted in *wholeness over hustle*— where you're no longer chasing achievement, but instead you're fully aligned and alive, finally free to rise to your greatest potential.

I have learned the magical secret of building stillness and personal fulfillment within the many moving parts of a high-achieving, high-responsibility life, and now I'm here to teach you to do the same.

Hustle will produce noise, but wholeness will produce legacy. And it all starts as we look within.

You see, deep down, I used to think that the more I did, *the more I would matter.*

The more I could achieve, *the more value I would hold in the eyes of others.*

The "better" I could be at doing a "good job" as a mom, as a business owner, and at every other role I was holding onto. . . *the more peace I would surely feel.*

Then I learned this truth: The pressure to achieve, to be more, and to do more will never offer the peace that can only be felt when you hold still long enough to see your own inherent worth.

I'm teaching you simple shifts that include an internal slowing down, a pattern of letting go, and the process of allowing enough space for your light to shine.

> The pressure to achieve, to be more, and to do more will never offer the peace that can only be felt when you hold still long enough to see your own inherent worth.

Just like a candle flickering in the wind will struggle to hold its steady light, your light and power within requires you to still the internal (and external) tumultuous swirl. Let's begin the journey to preserve your light.

*I'd recommend you pause right now to download the accompanying mini workbook for this chapter: www.mollyclaire.com/she-rises-workbook.

Overresponsibility: What We've Been Sold (and Bought Into Hook, Line, and Sinker)

As women, we have been conditioned to believe we should be everything to everyone. We were handed a story that we could "have it all," which actually meant that we should take on more responsibility than any human could possibly handle, with the hope of being valued by society. Having it all and doing it all is how we would prove our worth, our value, and how we would be allowed to claim a voice—and have some sense of power in our lives.

This has affected the way our brains are wired. Most women don't even think twice before taking on more responsibility. It's what a "good woman" does. It's how we are kind and feminine and lovely, living up to the societal standard of how a woman "should" be.

Consider a few statistics:

- A US-based study published in the *Journal of Marriage and Family* reports that **in most dual-income households, women carry between 65% and 73% of the mental load**—managing schedules, remembering appointments, anticipating needs, and holding the invisible architecture of daily life together.

- According to OECD-based data, **globally, women perform between 3 to 6 hours of unpaid labor per day,** while men contribute only 30 minutes to 2 hours. As a result, **working mothers are twice as likely as fathers to consider cutting back their work hours** due to the strain of childcare.

- This imbalance has real consequences. The Gender Equality Policy Institute cites that **women report up to 20% less free time than men, contributing to chronic overwhelm, diminished well-being, and long-term burnout.** The cost of this invisible labor is not just time—it's also vitality, ambition, and the ability to access the deeper parts of ourselves that thrive in rest, reflection, and creative spaciousness.

The worst part of all of this is that *it feels scary to take on less responsibility.* It literally creates fear in our body, activating the nervous system. You see, because we have been conditioned to believe that our value will increase when we take on more and "prove" ourselves, **to take on less is to risk being devalued, rejected, and ultimately feel emotionally unsafe.**

It's a pretty difficult position we find ourselves in: our nervous system feels safer in stress mode and over-responsibility, *while our soul, well-being, and light within are pleading with us to hold still.*

Rewiring our nervous system to feel safe taking on fewer responsibilities must be done intentionally. Allowing greater wholeness and the space for your light to shine is a decision. The stressed state from which most women operate comes at a cost. This cost impacts your well-being, limits your potential, and affects everyone and everything around you.

I want you to know this:

You are brilliant and you are capable.

You have enormous potential in every cell in your body.

However, if you're working on overdrive, the potency of your gifts, abilities, and impact cannot begin to be realized. Your unique genius within cannot shine in the way it's meant to shine. It's actually impossible. You can't be the "best" business owner, mom, friend, coach, leader, or anything else when you're suffocating in a state of stress day in and day out.

YOUR BRILLIANCE, YOUR GIFT, IS LIMITED BY HUSTLE

In my experience, both personally and with thousands of clients, you'll need some pretty compelling evidence to slow down your pace.

I've got evidence for you: some science, some practical real-life examples, and a little "woo," too. Are you ready for it?

Let's take the scientific approach first. The nervous system is the backdrop of all of your thoughts and emotions. When your nervous system is in a chronic stress state (sympathetic activation), your body prioritizes survival. When this happens, blood and energy are redirected to your survival systems and away from your prefrontal cortex. Your prefrontal cortex, which is responsible for high-level thinking, goes partially or fully "offline."

To be more specific, when you are in a state of stress, the part of your brain that allows you to plan ahead, prioritize, problem solve, emotionally regulate, control impulse, be creative, and engage in moral reasoning cannot properly function.

If you are someone who is high functioning in a high state of stress—*yes, I see you*—you may be thinking, *This doesn't really apply to me. Trust me when I say this does apply to you.* The science is clear. Don't be fooled by your "high functioning stress state."

Consider this: If you are this high functioning with such limited access to that prefrontal cortex, what is possible if you can maximize your brilliance?

The science is there—wholeness over hustle will expand your success. And taking the practical, real-world experience view also leads us to come to this same conclusion.

Let's shift gears now as we dive into two contrasting scenarios to illustrate the point. While you may not relate to these exact scenarios, please think of a personal scenario and see how this applies to you.

Scenario 1 (Cathy): A mom working from home; the sitter cancelled. She's got a toddler, a preschooler, and two elementary school-age kids.

Cathy's stress levels rise before she gets out of bed. She goes full force into the day; it feels like playing whack-a-mole. With each meltdown, every drink spilled, and all the "to-dos," she is trying to stay

> Consider this: If you are this high functioning with such limited access to that prefrontal cortex, what is possible if you can maximize your brilliance?

grounded. She's more reactive than she'd like to be (yes, she yells). She's trying to hold it together and moving through the tasks as fast as she can, just hoping that nothing falls through the cracks.

*Wow—can you feel the anxiety? I feel it just as I'm writing these words for you.

Scenario 2 (Tiffany): A mom working from home; the sitter cancelled. Same kids, same facts. However, *something is different within Tiffany.*

Tiffany knows her own inherent worth. She believes that her needs and well-being matter. She is gentle and kind with herself, believing that her brilliance can shine when she allows space for it. She knows that she is allowed to take up space. She has had the support and guidance to step into these beliefs and actually rewire her brain. She has different patterns in her nervous system. She has become a woman who flows through her day, embodying her own beautiful brilliance.

Here's how this plays out: Tiffany notices some stress as she begins the day, but, with mindfulness, it doesn't overtake her. She moves a bit slower and with more intention. This means she asks a bit more of her kids, enjoys interacting with them, and ends up taking on less. It feels easy and natural to do so. She's even able to feel some inspiration within her work projects, despite today's unexpected turn.

When emotions run high around her, Tiffany is able to emotionally regulate, thus co-regulating with her kids. This means that her kids are literally taking cues from her nervous system and emotional state that helps them stay more calm, too. Problems are solved more easily, creativity trumps catastrophizing, and, best of all, she is able to be present and in connection with her kids throughout the day. Equally, she sets healthy boundaries around her own space. She carves out adequate focus for work so she's not just checking boxes, she's creating brilliance.

Notice that people would label Tiffany as doing a "good job." In truth, both Cathy and Tiffany are doing the best they can within their own capabilities. Tiffany has simply had the support to cultivate a deeper sense of self. She has learned how to expand her emotional capacity. She has been guided to build internal wiring in her brain that creates a completely different but natural experience of life for her, and everyone benefits.

Okay, so now that we've checked the box on providing scientific evidence and a real-world example, it's time for "magic."

"Magic" is my favorite word to describe what can't be seen, but can be felt and known deeply. You may call it spirit, inspiration, light, or divinity. Whatever you call it, let's explore this awakening of the spirit together with my own personal example.

I felt so stuck in my business. I was doing everything I knew to do, but things just weren't landing with my audience; something was missing. At the same time, there was "magic" happening inside my work with my clients. Our work together allowed them to ignite their brilliance. As their mentor, I was holding space to give them permission, space to slow their pace, space to allow their ideal life and business flow to really matter. I was working with them on matters of the mind, emotion, self-connection, self-trust, and self-belief. This power was extraordinary, and their shifts were, too. Their deep transformations and the aliveness in them were palpable.

Ironically, I was the one feeling stuck, trying to figure out what was limiting the expansion of my work. *I knew that I needed to figure this out, and I needed to figure it out soon.* The old version of me would have worked harder. Over-extending myself, never taking a moment to rest until I had solved the problem. Thankfully, a wiser version of me now existed. A version of me that valued my own well-being and my need for rest. A version of me that was committed to giving myself a week of down time that I had promised myself. A version of me that said, "you are allowed to rest, you are allowed to be well, you are allowed to have fun, you are allowed to take care of your mental, emotional, and physical needs."

*This version of me was brought to the surface by my own deep work and exactly what I'm teaching you about today. The decision to **allow wholeness over hustle**. It was possible because of my own coach's side-by-side support. I'm grateful that we all benefit from guidance, coaching, support, and mental, emotional, and spiritual shifts that equip us to find a better way.*

In this moment of my life, as I offered myself the space and rest to reconnect with myself, calming the wind so my light could shine, it happened. While on my yoga mat, stretching and simply being present—"magic" flooded my heart and mind.

The words flew out of my mouth: "I need to offer a Master Coach Training. I've got to fill these tremendous gaps that exist for so many coaches. They are struggling—personally and professionally—and I know how to help them."

I could feel the tremendous power in what was about to transpire. In that next moment, as often happens, a critical voice in my head said, *Why you?*

Thankfully, my inner knowledge spoke up loud and clear, *Why not me?*

I knew my clients needed this help, and I was going to answer the call. That moment was made possible, not because of hustle, but because of greater wholeness.

That moment of "magic" is part of the reason this book is in your hands. Each of these women has trained with me to understand mind, body, and soul how to support their clients through deep transformation. They are brilliant, beautiful, and wise beyond comprehension. I'm so grateful to be a small part of watching their lights fully come to the surface.

When you are whole, you no longer fragment yourself for approval or speed. You become visible to the right people, opportunities, and the right ideas.

With 30 holistic master coaches now trained and certified (so far), this work moves forward, and this book is in your hands. These gifted and inspired women are sharing wisdom that now has a ripple effect.

As you can see, the "magic" is my favorite. The practical examples are powerful and tangible, and the science cannot be denied.

Are you bought in?

STILL THE WINDS, CLAIM THE LIGHT

In this last section of the chapter, I'm teaching you three key concepts to guide your next steps. These will be anchors for you as you transform toward *greater wholeness* and *next-level expansion of your potential.*

If you haven't yet, please take the time to download your free workbook at www.mollyclaire.com/she-rises-workbook. There, you'll find prompts and questions to help you personalize this work.

Concept #1 - Be gentle: The greatest power and light within you will come about as you are generously gentle towards yourself.

One of the biggest obstacles to exemplifying our own brilliance is the harsh, self-critical way in which too many of us approach life. "Setting a high standard" morphs into unfair and unattainable perfectionistic expectations of ourselves. "Going after your goals" becomes a pressure cooker of high performance and a fear of failure. The worry about "what people think" smothers our light.

The antidote to this is to be gentle with yourself, which begins with small steps to fully understand your inherent worth. It includes talking to yourself with kindness and compassion, increasing understanding of your own emotional needs, and attuning to the ways in which your mind, body, and soul need to be nurtured. In truth, this concept deserves an entire book of its own. But just a few small steps and the questions included in the workbook will get you well on the path forward.

Concept #2 - Make a choice: Wholeness begins with the choice to stay the course.

While you may be tempted to "go all in" and see this as a new checklist to achieve, that's not the path to this "success."

Instead, this path includes an invitation for you to commit to stay the course, while giving yourself plenty of permission. Permission to move at your own pace, or perhaps an even slower pace than that to which you're accustomed. Permission to take one small step at a time, with room for mistakes and setbacks. Permission to be a beginner—not knowing how to navigate this new version of life that includes more ease, enjoyment, and fulfillment.

This can feel challenging, as you'll likely feel uncertain and think you should be "getting there" sooner. Ultimately, I assure you, the gentle, forgiving, supportive pace will work. It's the secret. It's everything.

Concept #3 - Create and receive support: The right plan doesn't push, it supports. That's what makes lasting change possible.

One of the key concepts that I train my master coaches to implement is the designing of a plan for change that actually builds support. Instead of a list of "to-dos" that hold you accountable based on whether you're checking the boxes, supportive change means taking stock of what is needed for you to actually implement change easily. This means that, as you are working to rewire your brain, reset your emotional state, and completely shift internal patterns, you must understand what will get in the way and what will make those changes difficult.

You're allowed to make change easier for yourself, and it's more effective. It's the most soul-nourishing—and lasting—way to create change. Your plan must have personalized support, including mindset strategies, emotional processes, nervous system rewiring, and practical tangible strategies that will make change inevitable. The questions in the free workbook will help you to build your own plan—don't miss it.

THE FINAL WORD

You are destined for greatness. You have gifts within you that no one else possesses. You are unique and wise and gifted—it's only as you allow space for your light to shine brightly that the full impact of your abilities will be realized.

It all begins with understanding just how much you matter. Truly, knowing just how vital your existence is. It is your sacred opportunity to nourish your soul, mind, body, and spirit so your gifts within can be fully realized.

Please don't do this alone. We are wired for connection, and it's through connection that we grow, heal, and expand into the greatest version of ourselves. As you commit to this change, surround yourself with people who believe in you and lift you up. Allow people in your life to support you, compliment you, and speak life into you every day. Have a coach and mentor who will help you see the possibilities and open your eyes to the brilliance within you that you cannot quite see. You deserve all of the love and support as you truly become.

Thank you for giving us the opportunity to spend some time together. I'm grateful to be side-by-side with you on this journey.

CHAPTER 2

Discover Your True Self Through Doodles: Because Pens and Markers Are Cheaper than Therapy

Michelle Keil

"The Doodle Coach," Master Certified Holistic Coach, Doodling Instructor and Coach

🌐 thedoodlecoach.com

📷 instagram.com/michellekeilcoaching

f facebook.com/michellekeilcoaching

in linkedin.com/in/michelle-keil-350440221

Michelle Keil, affectionately known as "The Doodle Coach," is a master certified holistic coach and the creator of a unique coaching method who helps overwhelmed women quiet their inner critic, lighten their emotional load, and reconnect with who they truly are—through the surprisingly powerful tool of doodling.

Her playful yet profound approach is faith-centered, science and evidence-informed, and rooted in years of training, including an advanced certification in motherhood and family life. She weaves together creativity, faith, and nervous system-aware coaching to support women in finding grace in the margins of their lives.

Michelle's signature programs include "Drawn to Grace," a five-day guided doodle practice to build self-compassion, and "Draw Yourself In," a 12-week coaching experience for women ready to release perfectionism and rediscover their true voice. She also leads The Doodle Lab, a monthly creative space for reflection, connection, and nervous system regulation—no art skills required.

Whether through her courses, community, or one-on-one coaching, Michelle makes it safe—and even fun—for women to let go of who they think they *should* be and remember who they already are.

WHEN THE STRONG ONE GROWS WEARY

You're the glue holding everything together—meals, schedules, emotions. You manage meltdowns, soothe sibling squabbles, remember every dentist appointment, and somehow still pack a lunch with a note in it. You're the strong one. The dependable one. The one who gets things done. Everyone counts on you. But quietly, so quietly you may not even recognize it yet, you've grown weary.

It's not just physical exhaustion—it's emotional. Invisible. It's the weight of everyone else's needs, moods, and expectations resting silently on your shoulders. And then add the weight of your own expectations, judgments, and perfectionism. It's slowly burying you.

In the middle of it all, there's the soul-searching: *Who even am I anymore?*

A STATUE FORGOTTEN

Consider the story of **The Golden Buddha.**

In the heart of Bangkok, in 1935, a seemingly ordinary stucco statue of the Buddha was being relocated from its long-standing home at the abandoned Wat Phraya Krai temple. For nearly a century, this statue had stood quietly in the aging temple, its dull, gray exterior offering no clue of what lay beneath. The statue was transferred for safekeeping to a small, unassuming temple nearby: Wat Traimit.

For nearly twenty years, the statue sat there in silence, stored in a tin-roofed shed on the temple grounds—too large to ignore, too plain to revere. But that all changed in 1955.

The monks of Wat Traimit decided it was time to give the statue a more fitting home. A new building was constructed, and on May 25, 1955, they began the difficult process of moving the heavy figure—nearly ten feet tall and weighing over five tons—into its new space.

As workers attempted the final lift, something went wrong. The ropes snapped. The massive statue crashed to the ground. Dust flew. Stucco cracked. And in that moment, what seemed like a disaster revealed what no one could have imagined.

Beneath the broken exterior, a shimmering hint of something gold caught someone's eye.

Work stopped and discovery began. What followed was a careful, months-long unveiling. Piece by piece, the dull outer shell was removed. By December of that year, experts confirmed that hidden beneath the unassuming gray exterior was a solid gold Buddha, crafted centuries earlier and estimated to be worth millions.

It's believed that the statue had been covered in stucco by monks centuries ago to protect it from invading forces, its true value hidden in plain sight. And so it remained, patiently waiting to be discovered.

In February of 1956, the Golden Buddha was officially enshrined in its rightful place—no longer forgotten, no longer hidden.

Maybe you've been wrapped in your own version of stucco—layer by layer, year by year—until you barely remember what's beneath.

So many of us live with a layer of "stucco" covering our true selves, whether it be created out of fear, shame, expectation, or self-protection. We may look ordinary on the outside, and feel broken when we stumble or fall.

Somewhere along the way, you've lost your true self—not the version of you who manages everything, but the one beneath the surface. *The real you.*

COULD DOODLING REALLY HELP?

The idea of adding one more thing might seem laughable—especially something for yourself. Even more so, doing something as childish or frivolous as doodling.

Yet, what if this simple act could be a lifeline back to your true self? What if grabbing a pen for just five minutes a day could help you sort through the noise, lighten the emotional load, and reconnect with the woman underneath the roles?

"I don't like what I find when I slow down. I just see all the ways I'm falling short."

"My thoughts are too chaotic. I don't even know where to begin."

"But I'm a mess! I can't even think straight, let alone draw!"

That's a perfect place for doodling to begin. *No rules. No pressure. Just a pen, a page, and giving yourself permission* to show up as you are. It's not about being artistic. It's not about mastering a technique. It's about being honest.

YOU ARE THE GOLD

You were never lost. You were just covered up.

Take a breath here. Let that truth settle.

You are more than what you see. Your worth isn't defined by the layers that cover you, but in the divine brilliance beneath. And just like that golden statue, your true self is still there, patiently waiting to be uncovered.

Let's explore how this small, sacred practice can gently guide you back to your truest self.

LETTING IT OUT TO LET IT GO

You're not imagining it. Those layers are real.

This emotional load often goes unnamed. It builds up quietly in the background while you're doing everything you're "supposed to." You smile while your heart aches. You say "yes," when your heart is screaming *"no!"* You tell yourself you're fine, even when a part of you is whispering otherwise.

But here's the truth: *you weren't meant to carry it all.*

This is where doodling becomes more than just lines on a page. It becomes a sacred space—just in the *margins*—a gentle invitation to let go. When you doodle, you shift the emotional burden from *inside* your body to *outside* of it. What felt stuck and tangled starts to move. Thoughts you couldn't quite name find expression in color, shape, and movement.

> Your worth isn't defined by the layers that cover you, but in the divine brilliance beneath. And just like that golden statue, your true self is still there, patiently waiting to be uncovered.

Even if just for a moment, the page becomes a safe place to let thoughts and emotions out without judgment. A place where what you make, and you, don't have to be "pretty" to be accepted.

You're not expected to *fix* everything in five minutes of doodling. But you *are* allowed to set something down—to give your soul a breath and your heart a break. Let your pen and page carry what you no longer need to hold alone.

Each mark is a quiet reminder:

I don't have to carry all of this.
I can be gentle with myself.
I am allowed to feel, release, and rest.

When that burden starts to lighten, something else begins to stir. A gentle uncovering begins as you release some of the layers to the page. Compassion can start to grow, if you let it. Curiosity can be cultivated as you look at what is. This is where your healing starts, one quiet mark at a time.

SEEING THE SELF AGAIN: HOW DOODLING CAN REVEAL WHAT JUDGMENT TRIES TO HIDE

"I don't like what I find when I slow down. I'm too hard on myself."

Let's be honest: avoiding stillness is often about avoiding what you might find there. But here's the thing—you've already been carrying it. Doodling just gives it a safer place to land.

Many things help us see things differently. Take prescription eyeglasses, for example. Countless combinations of lenses adjust our vision so that we can see more clearly. As I have gotten older, my prescription has changed and, now, I need progressive lenses. These are made for multiple focal points to help me in different settings. I have one focal length that helps me to see in the distance more clearly. A second focal length helps me to read by focusing on the things that are closer to me.

I believe that the way we see things—our world, our experiences, our relationships, ourselves—is in large part influenced by the "lenses" we look through. These lenses are shaped by our beliefs and values—what is important to us and the thoughts we think over and over and over again. They are created over time by influences such as the culture we were raised in, our family of origin, education, religious upbringing, the experiences we have had, and the societal "norms" that we have picked up along the way.

Like lenses for the eyes, doodling becomes a lens for the soul. As you slow down and begin to see yourself again, doodling is a softer way to notice what lenses you might be wearing. You may even begin to notice the way those lenses are "coloring" your present experience. It is not about judgment; it is about noticing. Doodling allows you to look at yourself, not with criticism, but with curiosity. Not with harshness, but with wonder and compassion. You can wonder about what you doodle in a way you may not be willing to look at or wonder about yourself. It has a way of softening the edges of what you see. Doodling offers you the perspective of a mirror. It reflects the whole picture—the mess, the masterpiece, and everything in between. In the mirror, you notice the lenses you have on. Lenses you might not have realized are there because you have become accustomed to wearing them.

One session brought this concept to life in a real way:

I was working with a group of women and we were creating a doodle titled "This Is Me." On one side of our doodle self, we listed and doodled things we liked about ourselves, things we were proud of, and things we could give ourselves credit for.

I then instructed them to add the phrase, "**I love and accept myself**" on that side of the paper.

Then, on the other side of the page, we listed things we wished were different about ourselves, things we didn't like, things we wanted to change.

Again, I instructed them to add the phrase, "**I love and accept myself.**"

It was interesting to discuss together what our reactions were when I prompted them to write that phrase on their doodle. I don't know if any of us fully believe that phrase about the *good* things. And when it comes to the *bad* things, we question it even more.

How do all of these pieces of me EQUAL a me who is 100% worthy as is?

scattered

Hope

LOVE

Death & Loss

This is Me

Family

Broken

I love and accept myself

strong

Learning

creativity

anxiety despair grief

my mask

Pain

Judged

successes

I love and accept myself

Peace

Fear Loss Failure

growth

- emotional
- perfectionism
- judgmental
- self-critical
- hiding - masking

- Courage
- creativity
- compassionate
- adventurous
- listener

... and I am AMAZING! ♡

How could it be true that ALL of me is precious & important?

That doodle became more than a page—it became a mirror. One that helped us see that acceptance isn't about fixing what's wrong, but making space to love all of it.

It showed us something new about ourselves. Each of us is at a different place on that path, but we can see it is a path we are curious about. A path we want to explore a little more.

NAMING THE NOISE: YOUR LOUD (AND OFTEN RUDE) INNER CRITIC

One major source of emotional noise? That relentless inner voice that's always got something to say.

You might be thinking, like one of my clients, *My thoughts are too chaotic. I don't even know where to begin.*

You begin by identifying the voice that is holding you back from starting. The voice—or if you're like me, the entire cast of characters in your head—with the constant commentary. **That is not you.** That's the voice *about* you—not the voice *within* you. That's your inner critic, and the "lens" your inner critic is most often using is a magnifying glass. She zooms in on all your mistakes, missteps, and flaws until those are all you can see.

It is time to get to know her—and it's time you gave her a name. It's time to have a little fun! She may take on different personas depending on the day. . . or the pressure. Maybe your inner critic is like an *angry inner drill sergeant coach.* That relentless voice yelling from the sidelines. Always barking orders. Never satisfied, no matter how hard you try. Or perhaps your inner critic is like a *royal evil stepmother from fairy tales.* Always commenting on how common and worthless you really are. How you will never measure up. What if, even more confusing, your inner critic sounds like a *loving but over-protective parent?* Constantly scanning for danger or failure and catastrophizing what might happen. Overprotective and driven by fear, she shifts to self-blame when things go wrong.

Whatever type of inner critic you may have, she always wants the same thing: to protect you. She thinks that keeping you small will keep you safe. In her world, love is expressed as control, and protection is disguised as criticism. When you doodle your inner critic as a character, you move it from the shadows of your subconscious onto the page; you turn down the volume; you reclaim your sense of humor. You take away its power. You create space to breathe again.

So give her a name. Dress her up in a ridiculous outfit. Have some fun with this side of yourself. And if you need some inspiration, let me know. I can introduce you to some of mine:

"Tammi Toughlove"

"Marge McMotivator"

"Duchess Do-It-All"

"Queen Critiquealot" . . . The list goes on!

Remember, you are the gold beneath the layers you've used to protect yourself—perfectionism, people-pleasing, self-deprecation disguised as humility, self-criticism. Your inner critic is the clay. The doodle? It's your tool to chip away gently, one line at a time.

STARTING WHERE YOU ARE

So now, when you hear that voice saying, *But I'm a mess! I can't even think straight, let alone draw,* you can be a little more curious about *who* is really saying those things.

It's actually great! Start right there. Doodling is not powerful because it's polished. It's powerful because it's honest. The power lies in your willingness to meet yourself right where you are. You don't have to make sense. You don't have to be tidy. You just have to show up—with your pen, your breath, and your brave little heart.

Imagine a messy, cluttered room. This is the room where you have constantly stuffed everyone else's needs, priorities, and opinions. You've kept the door shut so no one sees. You don't even want to see. Doodling is like gently cracking that door open, looking in out of curiosity rather than shame. You don't have to clean the room all at once.

Just peek inside. Draw what you see.

Start gently sorting through it—not to "spring clean" your whole life. Just to softly acknowledge, *This is mine. This matters to me.* That's enough.

These are the sacred margins. Tiny pockets of time you can reclaim for yourself—not by clearing your schedule, but by reframing what's already there. The five minutes while the coffee brews. The carpool line. Between innings at the Little League game. Doodling in the margins isn't about adding more, but about making space.

THIS ISN'T JUST DOODLING—IT'S HOW YOU BEGIN TO BECOME

It's fair to ask: Can doodling actually shift something inside me?

Yes. Because this isn't about art. It's about access:

Access to self-compassion. Access to clarity. Access to healing.

When you draw from within, you reconnect with a different part of yourself. The "real you" can already be seen in full view. This is the invitation to become reacquainted with that part of yourself.

For many, it's easy to dismiss doodling as trivial when you're dealing with deep pain—grief, burnout, resentment. *It's not therapy. It's not a magic fix. But it is a doorway.* It opens a safe space where your soul can speak, to share what is already there. And sometimes, the act of slowing down, paying attention, and creating space may lead to surprising insights and healing.

I recently posed this question in my small group: "How have you recognized the impact of doodling?"

That's when a metaphor began to take shape. (Or is it an analogy? "Queen Critiquealot" has some notes for me!)

We began comparing the experience of self-awareness through doodling to different types of light. After some reflection, one image resonated deeply: doodling is like well-placed landscape lighting.

You don't always notice it right away. But it gently lights your path back to your true self.

Where other forms of coaching might bring self-awareness, like a flashlight illuminating your path, you may find you don't always have the flashlight with you. Or perhaps, you have forgotten to turn it on. Other self-awareness methods can feel more like a security floodlight that switches on at the slightest movement. The startling, bright light floods the area in such a way that you are momentarily blinded to your surroundings, and you actually "see" less than you did before.

While there may be a time and a place for each of those forms of "lighting," the gentler, consistent light of doodling seems to remain present for a longer duration without becoming overwhelming and without demanding more than you're ready to give.

What might happen if you give yourself just a little light today?

IN THE MARGINS, YOU'LL FIND HER

You don't need to fix yourself. You don't need to find some better version of you. The true you is already here. She's been under the surface all along, quietly waiting.

In the margins, you'll find her.

Doodling isn't about creating art; it's about creating space—for your thoughts, feelings, and healing. It may not be therapy, but it can be therapeutic. It's a doorway. A permission slip. A sacred invitation back to yourself.

You were never lost. You were just covered up.

....

In the margins, you'll find her.

....

You don't have to be an artist. You don't need fancy pens. You don't even need more time. You just need to be willing to show up and a pen that works.

So. . . pick up your pen. No pressure. No perfection. Find a scrap of paper. Let your hand move without judgment. Even one minute is enough.

Wanting to create a little "margin" for yourself as you begin? Reach out, and you can start this walk with a guide. Visit **thedoodlecoach.com** to arrange a complimentary "Margin Scribble Session" or to download the free guide: ***Grace In The Margins***.

Crack the clay. Let the gold shine through.

Because maybe the deepest healing doesn't happen in the loud or the dramatic—

but in the quiet margins,

where doodles become declarations,

play becomes prayer,

and your whole self is finally allowed to be seen.

Because maybe. . . just maybe. . . your truest self is only a few doodles away.

You're worth uncovering.

See what curiosity shows you.

In time, you will find gold.

CHAPTER 3

The Message in the Feeling

Carla Green

Master Life Coach

instagram.com/carlagreen.coaching

facebook.com/CarlaGreenCoaching

Carla Green is a master certified life coach who helps working parents shift from stress and survival mode into greater clarity, connection, and calm. Through a holistic blend of mindset work, nervous system support, and emotional awareness, she guides clients to stop overriding their feelings and start honoring them as powerful messages. Her coaching creates space for deep transformation—where pushing through is replaced by tuning in. Carla offers a grounded, nurturing presence that helps her clients reconnect with their inner wisdom and live with more peace and purpose. With compassionate guidance and practical tools, she empowers parents to reclaim their energy and presence so they can show up more fully—for themselves and the people they love.

• • •

If you're like most people, emotions are typically things you don't like to deal with. You don't mind positive ones, like happiness or amusement. Yet you usually notice the negative ones more, and you really don't like those ones. Have you ever considered that you are supposed to experience *all* of those emotions? You are *supposed to.* Your body was created to have all of these different feelings inside.

Have you ever asked yourself why you would have them? If you're a parent, you often wish that your kids wouldn't ever feel bad, especially so you don't have to deal with those emotions. You don't like the fits that they throw when they feel upset or the crying when they feel hurt. In yourself, you don't like feeling embarrassed when you make a mistake or feeling disappointed when something doesn't pan out. On a global scale, we don't like seeing others in pain or seeing them suffer, as it triggers something in us.

But what if those are all opportunities to learn something? What if you saw those emotions as messages and invited them in, rather than pushing them away?

If emotions are already happening in your body, meaning you are wired to experience them, then maybe you are *meant* to pay attention to them.

Think about a negative feeling you don't like to have. Stress. Anxiety. Disappointment. Sadness. Anger. Overwhelm. Fear. Nervousness. How does it feel in your body? Do you like how it feels? What do you do with it when it shows up?

If you're like most of us, you don't like how those feel in your body. You don't like feeling your heart racing, the teary feeling in your throat, the pressure in your chest, the tightness in your shoulders, the ringing in your ears, or the sweaty palms. So what do you do when they happen?

Maybe, like most human beings, you do whatever you can to make it go away. You eat. You ignore it. You try to talk yourself out of it. You distract yourself with something else. You scroll on your phone mindlessly. You shop. You procrastinate. You tell yourself you shouldn't be feeling this way: *What's wrong with me? Why can't I just get over it?* You blame someone else: *If they hadn't cut me off in traffic. . .*

Maybe that works—for a little while. Until it doesn't. So you do the same kind of thing the next time. And the cycle just continues. You keep trying to fix the feeling so no one has to feel badly—especially you.

But all that does is keep you chasing happiness and trying to control everything. That leads to burnout and frustration, not balance and peace.

This happened to one of my clients—let's call him John. He came to me feeling burned out and tired all the time. He wondered what was wrong, why he couldn't seem to find motivation for anything. At work, he was just coasting. He got tasks done, but didn't feel motivated to go above and beyond. He found himself often complaining with coworkers, dreading going to work, snacking mindlessly throughout the day to keep up some energy. At home, he was helpful, getting kids to activities and doing the dishes. But he still felt drained. He found himself indulging in late night snacks and staying up too late as he finally took time for himself, watching videos on topics that interested him. Then the morning would come too soon, and the cycle continued.

It wasn't that he didn't love his family or that he wasn't grateful for his job. He just didn't want to feel so depleted. He wanted to enjoy time with his kids more. He wanted more energy. He wanted to not dread work. He wanted to feel more connected to his wife. He wanted to have time for his interests. He wanted to feel something other than tired and stressed.

Maybe you feel that, too. You have gotten to a point in your life where you are just going through the motions. Where you are trying to chase more ease and happiness. Maybe you're wondering if you need a new job, city, routine, or parenting method just to feel better.

Like John, maybe you think your negative emotions are a problem to fix. That if you're feeling this way, something must be wrong with you.

Now, of course, your physical health matters. That does play a role in how we feel overall and in our mental and emotional capacity. If you feel the need to visit your doctor or get labs done, do it. And if working out helps, keep it up.

But what if you've tried those things and still feel stuck? You can't seem to get out of this rut. You can't seem to stick to a workout routine. You can't seem to enjoy your life or manage your stress anymore. You can't seem to feel better no matter what you try. What if the missing piece is how you respond to your emotions?

WHAT ARE EMOTIONS AND WHY THEY MATTER

Emotions are simply sensations or "vibrations" in your body. When your brain has a thought or notices something around you, it releases chemicals, and your body responds. Research has found that when we allow ourselves to experience these sensations instead of fighting them, they often pass in about 60-90 seconds.

When you understand that, you can look at *why* you might be experiencing it. Instead of ignoring the emotion, distracting yourself from feeling it, yelling because of it, or blaming yourself or anyone else for how you're feeling, you are able to notice the emotion and get curious about it. You stay calm and start to see how the emotion could actually be here to help you. You ask yourself what the cause might be, and then decide what you want to do next. This process—getting curious—is what leads to growing your emotional capacity and emotional maturity. It is what opens you up to more peace, more presence, and more enjoyment in your life.

Let's go back to John's experience. We looked at what he felt most often and what he did in response. Stress and frustration were the two predominant emotions, and he often found himself mindlessly reaching for something to eat. I encouraged him to notice when he would do that and then ask himself, *What do I need right now?* The common answer was that he needed a quick break and recharge of energy. We brainstormed other options for what he could do instead of snacking. As he began implementing those ideas more often, he noticed his energy coming back.

We talked about how those feelings were messages from his body that he needed something, like little red warning flags popping up. We discussed how feeling stress and frustration didn't mean he was doing anything wrong, that his job was wrong for him, or that his boss was to blame. They were simply little messages saying, "Hey! There's something we need."

Here's a metaphor I often use: think about a toddler who wants your attention. Your toddler will say, "Mommy, Mommy, Mommy. . ." until they get it. If they don't get it right away, they usually get louder. They follow you everywhere. They may even start getting upset and tug and pull on you, or kick and scream until they get what they want. If we look at what's happening, that toddler is simply asking for some time and the attention they need. But if they get ignored for too long, they start taking matters into their own hands to get what they want.

It's the same with your emotions. They will keep showing up louder and louder until they get your attention. They can show up as a yelling match with your spouse, apathy for things you used to enjoy doing, or as illness. The interesting thing is that emotions don't need a long time to be addressed. When acknowledged, they usually last less than 90 seconds in your body. When you understand that, you don't need to be afraid of allowing your emotions. They are there for a reason. And in the long-run, it is much better to tend to them early on than to let them go unnoticed and intensify. Those chemicals need to be flushed out of your system, not stopped up, where they can cause more damage.

You may be thinking now, *Great! I'll hurry up and feel an emotion so I can get rid of it.* Let me caution you: the point isn't to *get rid* of emotions. They don't fully leave you if they aren't properly given the attention they need. Just like the toddler, if you say, "Yes, honey, okay, in one second," the toddler may be appeased for a moment, having had a bit of attention. But as any parent knows, that doesn't last long before the toddler once more takes matters into their own hands. Or they learn that they will be ignored no matter what, to the point they stop asking. Neither of those outcomes are good. You want to feel the full range of emotions because you want to live a rich, full life.

My client Evan learned this. As an executive in his company, he was dealing with a lot of pressure. One time in particular, he had an intense interaction with a coworker that left him feeling extremely frustrated and defensive. As we had been working together for a few months by this time, he was familiar with acknowledging his emotions rather than ignoring them. However, he found that as he tried to move forward, he kept getting snagged by this same frustration and defensiveness. In our next meeting together, I asked him if he had let himself sit with the emotions. He admitted that while he had tried to learn from the experience, he hadn't actually spent time with the emotions. We paused in session to do a body scan. Eyes closed, he breathed deeply and noticed where the tension lived. He began to relax and felt the tension

> You want to feel the full range of emotions because you want to live a rich, full life.

run out of his chest and jaw. Afterward, he said, "I didn't realize I was still holding on to that."

> Emotions are messengers. They carry valuable insight if you're willing to listen.

We explored what those emotions were trying to tell him. He gained more clarity and peace and knew how he could move forward more intentionally.

Emotions are messengers. They carry valuable insight if you're willing to listen. Things like, "There is something you need right now." "This means a lot to you." "You're feeling nervous because you don't want to disappoint anyone." "You are avoiding it because you don't want to feel embarrassed." "You really care about them a lot and don't want to see them hurt." Emotions help you understand what you need and how to connect more deeply.

WHAT TO DO WITH THESE EMOTIONS

You may be thinking, *Okay, but what do I actually* do *with all this?* I'm not here to convince you—but I do invite you to try it. Doing it is the best way to experience the magic of your emotions.

Start by asking yourself: What three emotions do I feel most often? Are they emotions that help me move forward, or are they ones I would rather not feel? What would I be able to do if I didn't feel them so much? Would I be willing to take 30-60 seconds to allow these emotions to move through me instead of stopping them? What if doing so meant I could live with more ease and more energy?

Let's try it. Notice what you are feeling right now. Then take 60 seconds to try this quick body scan:

Close your eyes. Place your hands on your heart. Breathe slowly and steadily. Moving from head to toe, take notice of how your body feels. Notice any sensations like tension, tightness, buzzing, bubbling, swirling, bouncing. . . Notice the speed of the sensation and its temperature. Notice whether it gets more intense or it starts to subside. Notice if it moves to different places in your body. No words needed. No judgement. Just observe. Breathe. Once it feels as though it may have softened or passed, take a deep breath. Open your eyes.

Good job! That was allowing an emotion. Not too bad, right?

Now ask yourself: *What is that feeling about? What is it trying to teach me? What is it here to say?* Sometimes you will have a clear answer right away, and sometimes the answer will take a little longer to reveal itself. Allow for all of it.

You can do this exercise anytime and with any emotion. It may feel awkward at first. That's okay, let it. Just like anything new, it's going to feel awkward and unfamiliar. But the more you practice it, the easier it becomes.

If you'd like help getting started, I have two free tools for you: a short guided audio body scan and a printable reflection guide with simple steps. You'll find them at bit.ly/emotiontools.

Now, you may be thinking, *I don't have time to do this.* That's what my client Samantha said, too. "I have kids who need my attention and dishes to do and carpools to drive and church assignments to complete and meals to make. . . I can't stop to process my emotions when I'm feeling them."

As we talked through her concerns, I pointed out that it might not be necessary to do this full, eyes-closed process every time, right in the moment. Certainly, as your child is throwing a fit and you feel anger bubbling up in you, it may not be the ideal moment to pause to complete this full exercise. Instead, you can do a quicker version in the moment, and save the full process for later when you have more time.

It might look like this: Your child is throwing a fit in the grocery store. You feel yourself getting more agitated as it continues. You notice your body tightening and heating up. You take a moment to breathe slowly and remind yourself this is just an emotion in your body, just vibrations. You remember your child is just doing what children do sometimes, because they are still learning how to express their emotions in a calm way. You breathe through your emotions. The result? You're able to remain calm and help your child the way you *want* to. The icing on the cake is you show your child by example that feelings are not bad to have, how to process emotions, and how to express them appropriately. You model emotional regulation in real life.

This only takes seconds. Your brain works fast. It's about pausing long enough to stay in the driver's seat.

As you go through this process, you may wonder whether it's necessary to label the emotion. No, it's not. Your body works through feeling, through sensations. It doesn't need your mind to give it words in order to feel. That being said, sometimes your brain really wants something to think about. You may find it chattering as you try this process, and that's okay. Just gently draw your attention back to your body. Let the words happen afterwards as you ask yourself questions about what your body is trying to tell you.

Try it out! See what opens up for you!

Remember, you were created to feel—a full, rich life includes the full range of emotions. There is so much available to you! More peace, more energy, and more love are all within reach. Everything you need is already within you. You don't need to fix yourself. You just need to listen. Your emotions are here to help you live a life you love. After all, emotions are the language of your inner wisdom. Invite them in as friends waiting to tell you something, and you will experience their magic and power as you create a beautiful life you will love.

You've got this!

CHAPTER 4

Grieving and Growing: How to Rebuild Life After the Unthinkable

Margo Fordonski

Master Certified Holistic Life Coach and Grief Educator

Margofordonski.com

linkedin.com/in/margo-fordonski-033b27a6

instagram.com/margofordonski_lifecoach

facebook.com/margofordonskilifecoach

Margo Fordonski is a master certified life coach, certified grief educator, and a twice-bereaved parent. After losing both of her children—most recently her son, Andrew, who lived with brain cancer for 24 years—Margo has walked the long, complex path of grief firsthand. Her personal journey led her to a powerful calling: to support other mothers navigating life after the unthinkable.

Margo helps grieving moms find peace, resilience, and renewed hope—not by "moving on," but by learning how to carry their grief with love. Her one-on-one coaching approach is deeply personalized, meeting each mother where she is with compassionate guidance and tools that support nervous system regulation, emotional processing, and holistic healing. She guides her clients in healing at their own pace, rediscovering who they are now, and gently rebuilding a life that honors both their child and their continued growth.

Her work is trauma-informed, heart-led, and rooted in the belief that grief is not something to fix—it's something to tend to with care, courage, and support. Through her coaching, writing, and lived witness, Margo offers a safe and understanding space for grieving moms to feel less overwhelmed, more connected to themselves, and begin to rebuild a life that holds both sorrow and joy.

THE UNTHINKABLE

Perhaps you, too, have experienced the unthinkable—a loss so great that you can hardly wrap your arms around it. If I could whisper something to you now, dear reader, it would be this: You are not alone.

It was 4:45 a.m. when my son Andrew took his last breath. After 24 years of fighting brain cancer with indescribable courage, he finished his work here on Earth. His final sixteen hours were harrowing, a stretch of suffering I was powerless to stop. I had been awake since Wednesday morning. It was now Saturday. I was traumatized, guilt-ridden, and shattered.

The room was dark. It was so quiet—a kind of silence I had never known before. Then, as morning began to break, the birds started to sing. I remember being stunned that the sun had the audacity to rise, that the world would keep turning when my world had just ended.

In the early days, grief overwhelmed every part of me. I replayed his final hours on repeat. My body was flooded with panic. I cried constantly. I couldn't focus, couldn't read, couldn't escape the memories or the guilt. How had it gone so wrong? I had been his nurse, his advocate, his world—why couldn't I protect him in the end?

I no longer recognized myself. Once capable, strong, and calm under pressure, I had become anxious, avoidant, overstimulated, and afraid. I could suddenly come and go without arranging care— but I didn't want to go anywhere. The silence of my freedom was deafening. I had lost my child. And I had lost myself.

People meant well, but their words often hurt. "He's in a better place." "Now you can focus on yourself." "You should come to this retreat—get away." I wanted to scream. I wanted to be alone. I wanted my son back.

In those early days, pain was the only thing that kept him close. Letting go of the pain felt like letting go of him. And yet—slowly, gently—I began to meet other grieving mothers who were a little farther down the path. Was it really possible to survive this?

If I could whisper something to you now, dear reader, it would be this: You are not alone. The way you feel right now will not last forever. No emotion is permanent. Grief comes in waves, and every single feeling you are having is normal. Someday, there may be room for more than pain. There may be room for peace.

Love never ends.

YOU ARE NOT BROKEN

Grief is not a problem to be fixed. It's a sacred process to be honored.

In the early days after Andrew died, I expected our family to grieve together, just as we had lived through cancer together. We had been by his side through every scan, surgery, and setback. We were all there in his final hours. I thought surely we would carry the weight of his absence the same way. But that didn't happen. I was unprepared for how differently the loss of Andrew would affect each of us. So many families expect to grieve as one, especially after caregiving together, but grief is individual, not collective.

> Grief is not a problem to be fixed. It's a sacred process to be honored.

What followed was nothing like what I imagined grief "should" look like. I cried more than I ever knew was humanly possible. I couldn't be in my own house—it had become the scene of the worst thing that ever happened. The hospital bed in the family room was gone, but I could still see it. I couldn't think straight. I couldn't read. Crowds and noise triggered panic attacks. My nervous system felt completely unregulated. I didn't trust how I would respond to anything—everything felt unsafe, unfamiliar. And soon, I began to wonder: What's wrong with me? When am I going to go back to my old self?

This is what I now know: Nothing was wrong with me. And nothing is wrong with you.

What you're feeling isn't weakness; it's love in its rawest form. You're not broken—you're grieving. Grief is not something you "get over." It's something you learn to make space for. It becomes part of you—not all of you—but a thread in the fabric of your life now.

So many grieving moms carry the silent weight of unrealistic expectations. *I should be better by now. I shouldn't still be crying every day. I'm stuck. I'm going backwards. Nobody understands me.* But grief isn't linear. It doesn't follow neat stages or timelines. It's more like a wave—sometimes it crashes into you and knocks you down, and other times it gently laps at your feet. Either way, it's still grief. And all of it is valid.

I carried unbearable guilt about Andrew's death—that he suffered, that I missed something, that I should have been able to make it easier. I see the same torment in many of my clients: guilt, anger, blame, the belief that pain is the only way to stay connected to their child. But the truth is, *love is what keeps the connection alive.* As one of my mentors, David Kessler, says, "Healing does not mean forgetting. It means remembering with more love than pain."

When I work with grieving moms, I help them begin to meet themselves with compassion. To stop trying to go back to who they were before. To start exploring who they are now—a mother who is still loving, still longing, still living. You invite your child into the present: through flannel shirts worn like hugs, heart-shaped rocks found on a walk, signs that show up when they need them most. You make space—not just for grief, but for restoration, too. A journal. A breath. A walk in the sun. A moment of peace.

This is the heart behind a free guide I created called "10 Comforting Rituals for Moms to Support Your Nervous System Through Grief—Practical Things You Can Do Every Day." These rituals are gentle, simple, and helpful in the earliest weeks of grief, and many continue to be daily anchors on the healing journey. You can find this guide at either margofordonski.com or https://www. margofordonski.com/freeguide.

To the mom who feels broken: I've been where you are—the dark night of the soul. You are not broken. You do not need to be fixed. You are grieving. And healing is possible. You don't have to do it alone.

THE ONLY WAY OUT IS THROUGH

One of the most important things to understand is this: Grief doesn't end. There is no finish line. No "after" where grief neatly disappears. Many people come to grief support or coaching believing that acceptance is a final destination—like reaching the end of a race. But grief isn't a race. It's a lifelong relationship with something you cannot change.

If grief is the natural human response to loss, and the loss is permanent, then of course the grief will remain with us in some way. What changes over time is how you relate to it. *The goal isn't to get rid of grief, but to integrate it, carry it forward, and choose how you respond to it—on purpose.*

You don't move on from grief. You move with it.

It becomes part of the fabric of your life—woven into everything you are and do. Grief can show up in many ways: numbness, emotional swings, exhaustion, foggy thinking, even physical pain. If you don't understand this, you might begin to believe there's something "wrong" with you.

The grief model that has been most transformative for my own healing, and the one I teach most often, is the "dual process model" developed by Margaret Stroebe and Henk Schut. It's simple, generous, and validating, offering a roadmap for integrating restorative activities alongside all-consuming grief and daily obligations. It says healing happens through intentional movement between two types of experiences:

Loss-oriented activities are things that bring us directly into contact with our grief: crying, remembering, talking about our loved one, journaling, handling logistics, honoring anniversaries. These help us process pain and acknowledge the reality of the loss.

Restoration-oriented activities are everything else: distraction, hobbies, walks, Netflix, laughter with a friend, playing pickleball, getting through your to-do list, having a moment of peace. These give the brain and body a break.

You go back and forth, like a pendulum or a ping-pong ball. One moment, you're crying. Next, you're laughing. Then back to grief. Then out again. This back-and-forth isn't avoidance—it's necessary.

This model helps dismantle one of the biggest myths about grief: that you're only doing it "right" if you're actively grieving all the time. That if you laugh, smile, or forget for a little while, you must not be grieving enough. But healing requires breaks.

Let me share a moment that shifted everything for me. The summer we moved, a neighbor invited me to play pickleball. I avoided it for months. Finally, I agreed—just to stop the invitations. We got to the court, started learning the rules, hitting the ball, keeping score. An hour went by, and I realized I hadn't thought about Andrew once.

My brain had been so focused on the game, I'd gotten a break from my own grief. I came home feeling a kind of peace I hadn't felt in ages. The grief was there, ready and waiting to be picked up again, but for a brief time, I was able to get relief from the pain—a break I didn't know was possible, much less how much I needed it. I found that little slice of relief allowed me to handle the harder parts a little more easily.

That one experience gave me hope—hope that I could do something I enjoyed, that I could connect, that I might someday truly love my life again. Not just survive it. Pickleball became a regular part of my healing. My husband joined, we made new friends, and I eventually started playing in tournaments. What began as a distraction became a doorway back to myself.

That is dual processing. A break, a breath, a window, followed by space to grieve again, when needed. Grief is not all-or-nothing. It is a dance between loss and life. Between sorrow and sunlight. Every time you step into a moment of connection, creativity, rest, or peace, you are not moving on. You are moving forward. With love. With memory. With resilience. With hope.

I had a client who was struggling with how to incorporate restorative activities into her days. She didn't even know what they could be or when she'd have time for them. Together, we brainstormed simple possibilities—a morning cup of tea in silence, a ten-minute walk, calling a friend who made her laugh. Then we created a gentle schedule, mapping out when she might try these activities during her week. We also scheduled specific time for her grief work—journaling, looking at photos, allowing the tears.

This practice of anchoring her week with both restoration and grief began to create the breaks she desperately needed. She started experiencing the mental rest that helped her carry the harder parts a little more easily. The dance between loss and life became intentional rather than chaotic.

WHEN THE POSSIBILITY OF LIFE AFTER LOSS BEGINS TO RETURN

Around the five-year anniversary of Andrew's passing, I hit a wall. It felt like a significant milestone, but inside, I was discouraged and flat. I was managing the day-to-day tasks, and from the outside, it probably looked like I was doing okay. People told me I was strong. But inside, I felt hollow. I began to wonder if this was it—if this numb, going-through-the-motions version of life was all that was left for me.

That's when I signed up for a grief retreat being held on a lake in Wisconsin, about an hour from where I grew up. My anxiety was still intense at the time, so my husband flew with me to Chicago and drove me to the retreat. Something inside me knew I had to be there. It felt like my future depended on it.

At the retreat, one of the activities was to create a vision board—something I hadn't done or even considered doing since Andrew died. I hadn't allowed myself to think about the future, let alone imagine a life I might want to create. But something shifted as I flipped through magazines and clipped out images and words that resonated with me. Slowly, a vision started to emerge—one that felt light and peaceful, filled with connection, purpose, and possibility.

Tears come to my eyes even now as I remember that weekend. Because the life I'm living today mirrors so much of what I placed on that board. That retreat was my ray of light. It didn't erase my grief, but it showed me that maybe—just maybe—healing was possible. That I wasn't doomed to live in suffering forever.

One of the heaviest parts of my grief was the guilt I carried. Life was easier in some ways without the daily caregiving, the constant medical appointments, and the financial strain. I could come and go more freely, and yet that freedom felt like betrayal. How could I enjoy this new life when the only reason it was easier was because Andrew wasn't here?

A fellow bereaved mom asked me, "What would Andrew want for you?" That simple question stayed with me. I thought about my beliefs, about heaven and peace and the release from suffering. I realized Andrew no longer had to endure pain, and maybe, just maybe, I didn't have to, either. That was the beginning of releasing some of the guilt I held so tightly.

I stopped resisting what was. Andrew had finished his work here. I was still here, and I had more to do.

I began choosing thoughts and words intentionally. Instead of saying, "I'll never be okay," I tried, "Healing is possible." I started creating moments of peace on purpose. Instead of letting grief and life happen to me, I chose to take an active role in shaping what came next.

Rediscovering who I was outside of being Andrew's mom and caregiver didn't come easily. I had spent much time focused on his needs that I forgot what I even liked to do. At first, it was easier to start with what I didn't want. Slowly, through trial and error, I uncovered things that brought me joy again.

On a trip to San Diego with my husband and two adult children, we rented bikes and rode along the path on Coronado Island. As I watched them ride ahead of me, I realized this was our first ever family bike ride. Andrew couldn't ride a bike, so we had never done that before. It was bittersweet—but also healing. I wanted more of those moments with my kids.

We bought bikes. We went on more rides. I said "yes" to new experiences and learned to pay attention to what truly felt good—not what I "should" do, but what aligned with who I was becoming.

Coaching helped me get there. Having a safe, supportive space to explore my thoughts and feelings, to reconnect with my values, to identify what mattered most—it changed everything. Journaling became a powerful tool. So did being in community with other grieving moms. The relationships I've built through grief are some of the most meaningful of my life.

Eventually, my own transformation inspired me to become a coach. I became a certified life coach, then a master coach, and a certified grief educator. Now I help other moms rebuild after loss. My mission is to walk with them as they grieve fully and live fully.

Grief doesn't shrink. But you grow around it. That's the truth no one tells us. Integration—not elimination—is the way forward. You don't have to get over your grief. You get to build a life around it, one that reflects your values, your hopes, and your love.

People tend to believe that grief shrinks over time

What really happens is that we grow around our grief

Lois Tonkin's Model – 1966 "Growing around Grief"

This is what it means to grow after loss. Not to forget or move on—but to move forward, on purpose, with love.

REBUILDING WITH LOVE, NOT IN SPITE OF IT

Even if you can't see it yet, I want you to know this: There is light ahead.

Not the kind that erases grief or fixes what can never be undone, but a softer, gentler light. The kind that peeks through the cracks. A light that makes space for both sorrow and beauty. A light that says: there can still be moments of peace. Of meaning. Of joy.

> **Grief does not mean your story is over. It means the story is continuing in a new way.**

You don't have to choose between love and loss, grief and gratitude, remembering and rebuilding. You are allowed to hold all of it. To ache and still laugh. To miss them and still move forward. To cry when their song plays—and smile, too, because you can still feel them dancing with you in the kitchen. This is not moving on. This is living forward with love.

Grief does not mean your story is over. It means the story is continuing in a new way. A way in which your child is still a part of your life, woven into your days not just in memory, but in meaning. You carry them with you—in your heart, your choices, your tears, your laughter. In the way you show up. In the way you love others. In the way you begin to love yourself again.

Healing doesn't mean the pain disappears. It means you learn to live beside it. To grow a life around it. To create something meaningful not in spite of your grief, but through it.

This is the kind of healing that's possible. The kind that honors the love that will never end. *You are not broken. You are grieving. And you are growing.*

You don't have to be ready for the whole path. Just the next small step. And then the one after that. There is no rush. No right way. There is only your way—and the quiet knowledge that, even now, even here, life is still worth living. Not because it's easy. But because it's yours.

And because *love never ends.*

CHAPTER 5

Mirror, Mirror on the Wall. . . What the Heck Happened?: Stepping into Your Worth as a Woman of a "Certain Age"

Jackie Swainson

Master Certified Life Coach, Speaker, Workshop Presenter, Board Governance Advisor

jackieswainsoncoach.com

mollyclaire.com/directory-of-life-coaches

instagram.com/jackieswainsoncoach

facebook.com/Jackieswainsoncoach

Jackie Swainson is a master certified holistic coach with experience in trauma, family, and relationships with a focus on midlife transitions and changes. For the last five years, she has worked with women who feel like they are standing at a crossroads with no idea which way to go.

She works to help you discover who you are today, not try and return who you were at thirty. You'll start to see yourself differently, noticing visible outer and inner changes, understanding that you can create who you want to be, let go of beliefs that no longer serve you, and transition into the graceful authentic woman of "a certain age" that finds life a joy.

Midlife doesn't have to be an ending. It can be a beginning. As a woman of faith who has spent a good deal of time in the messy middle of this transition, Jackie has developed a way to help you recreate, redesign, and reignite your life. This new chapter can be full of joy and meaning. She guides you with understanding, compassion, experience, and lots of laughter through the doubt and helps you create your own new road.

• • •

I t always starts out innocently enough.

You're just brushing your teeth in the morning, bleary-eyed and barefoot, when your gaze drifts up to the mirror and suddenly you stop mid-brush. Who is that? When did your neck start doing that thing? Why are your eyebrows now attempting a dramatic exit stage left? And when, dear heavens, did your upper arms become audition-worthy for a Jell-O commercial?

"Mirror, mirror on the wall," you mutter, "what the actual heck happened?"

Midlife sneaks up on us like a well-meaning aunt who shows up uninvited and insists on rearranging your furniture. It's not that you weren't warned. But no one quite prepared you for the moment you'd look in the mirror and not just see crow's feet, but entire avian colonies nesting around your eyes. Or that you'd start scanning restaurant menus based on what wouldn't give you heartburn. Or that you'd forget what you were saying mid-sentence. . . again.

....

Midlife isn't a crisis. It's a "cracking open."

....

What seems to be falling apart is really the start of something remarkable. This "what the heck happened" moment? It's your soul knocking—maybe gently, maybe with a full-on battering ram—inviting you into a new, deeper, bolder chapter of becoming.

You've spent decades doing the things you were supposed to do—pleasing people, raising families. Building careers, saying yes when you wanted to say no, saying no to dessert when you really wanted cake. You've been dutiful daughters, dependable partners, attentive mothers, loyal employees, and community glue sticks. You've shown up. You've powered through. You've kept the wheels turning and people fed.

And somewhere in that mix, you might have forgotten how to hear yourself. Or you've heard yourselves faintly and told that voice to wait until after the soccer season. Or menopause. Or retirement. Or the next round of dental bills.

Well, my friend, now is the time.

Midlife isn't a crisis. It's a "cracking open." And what's underneath that old script—once you peel it back with curiosity and maybe some chocolate—is a woman of wisdom, grit, humour, and untapped potential just waiting to strut out in leopard print and claim some serious space.

So, let's talk about who you really are becoming—and how wildly worth it that woman is.

OWNING THE TRANSITION

There's a moment, somewhere between switching to sensible shoes and then to pants with elastic waists, when you start to wonder: Is this just how it is now? Is this the slow fade into beige cardigans and lukewarm tea?

Let me be clear: midlife is not a disappearing act. It's not the slow retreat into irrelevance that culture has tried to sell you. It's not the time to shrink, fade, or settle. No ma'am. It's the time to own the transition and rewrite the narrative.

The truth is that society doesn't quite know what to do with women of "a certain age." We're not young enough to be marketable in their glossy magazines, and not old enough to be revered as wise women on a mountaintop (though we could absolutely rock the robe and big stick if necessary). Instead, we are often painted with vague, patronizing strokes—"still vibrant," "gracefully aging," "holding up well."

Let me tell you what you're *really* doing: you're becoming. Sharpening. Shedding. Standing. There is a power in this stage of life that isn't loud or performative—it's deeper, grounded, and unbothered. It comes from knowing what matters and what can kindly see itself out.

Yes, our bodies are changing. Yes, we may now need a magnifying mirror, readers, and possibly a Sherpa to help us put on a sports bra. But we also have a perspective we never had at 25. We've got the receipts—literal and emotional—for all the roads we've traveled, and we are still standing.

Owning the transition means saying: I'm not going back. I'm not trying to be who I was. That woman served her purpose, and I honor her. But now, I'm giving myself permission to be who I'm meant to be next.

That's the plot twist most of us don't see coming. Midlife doesn't shrink us unless we let it. In fact, this is the first time many of us have had the space to ask, "What do I want?" Not "what's expected" or "what keeps the peace," *but what sets my soul on fire?*

Owning the transition also means you stop apologizing. For taking up space. For resting. For having options. For changing your mind. For wanting more.

It's not a crisis, it's a crossing. A rite of passage. And like all good crossings, it's a little disorienting at first. The maps don't always match the terrain. But the compass—your intuition, your voice, your hard-earned wisdom—is strong.

This is your invitation: Step boldly into the shift. Let the world adjust to you. And if it doesn't? Adjust your heels, your boundaries, and your lighting—and carry on anyway.

THE BELIEFS WE OUTGROW

Beliefs are sneaky little things.

We pick them up early—like emotional hand-me-downs—and wear them for decades, never stopping to ask if they fit anymore. Some of them were useful, once. They kept us safe, helped us succeed, or made people like us. But just like you wouldn't still be wearing your prom dress to a dinner party today, some beliefs are meant to be outgrown.

Midlife is the ideal time to step into the metaphorical closet of your mind, hold up each belief, and ask: Does this still serve me? Or is it time to donate this one to the Great Cosmic Thrift Store?

Let's name a few of the classics many of you have carried for far too long:

1. **"I need to make everyone happy."** Bless our hearts, we tried. We became emotional contortionists—twisting, shrinking, smoothing things over—just to avoid discomfort. But people-pleasing is exhausting, and spoiler alert: It doesn't please anyone in the long run. Especially not us.

2. **"If I don't do it, it won't get done."** Somewhere along the line, you were handed the belief that your value came from being perpetually responsible for all the things, all the people. But now? You get to decide what really deserves your energy. Hint: It's not everyone else's laundry or unprocessed feelings.

3. **"It's too late for me."** This one's a heartbreaker. The idea that you missed your shot. That your best days are behind you. Nonsense. You're not too late—you're seasoned! There are dreams with your name on them that couldn't have been pursued until now because you hadn't yet become the woman strong enough to carry them with clarity and passion.

4. **I'm not allowed to want more."** Oh yes you are! Wanting more of anything—peace, purpose, joy, visibility—is not selfish. It is sacred. Women of a "certain age" are allowed to have ambition, desire, curiosity, and cravings (and not just for chocolate or a nap).

These outdated beliefs might have gotten you here, but they won't take you to where you're going next. And the good news? Beliefs are not facts. They are stories. And stories can be edited, rewritten, or left on the cutting room floor altogether.

So, what if, instead, you believed:

*I am allowed to take up space.

*I get to trust my own timing.

*I am just getting started.

Here's the thing: You don't need to have it all figured out. You just need to be more willing to question the scripts you've been handed—and choose new ones that feel more like freedom.

It's not about reinventing yourself. It's about remembering who you were before the world told you who to be.

I coached Janet for 18 months before she had her "aha" moment. It wasn't earth shaking, but a building realization that she wasn't late for anything. She had arrived just at the perfect moment of understanding that she was ready to become who she always wanted to be. . . herself. Not the version she was supposed to be, or what her family expected her to be. Her life became hers again and she hasn't looked back.

ADJUSTING TO CHANGE

Change, you are told, is the only constant, but that doesn't mean it ever stops feeling like an ambush.

One minute you're breezing through life with a color-coded calendar and tight glutes, and the next, your metabolism ghosts you, your kids leave the house, and you're crying at insurance commercials while Googling "normal swelling after 50."

Change in midlife isn't always dramatic. Sometimes it's subtle—your tolerance for nonsense drops, your attraction to drama-free friendships increases, and you start saying things like, "I can't go out tonight, I've already taken off my bra." That, too, is change. And it matters.

But real talk: change is uncomfortable. Not because you're weak or resistant, but because it asks you to leave behind what you knew—and who you thought you were. It forces you to sit in the messy middle between old roles and new rhythms. And for women who've spent decades being the steady hand in everyone else's chaos, sitting in our own uncertainty can feel unnerving.

So how do we adapt?

First, we stop trying to control the tide. Midlife is not a project to manage, it's an ocean to swim. The more we try to cling to what was—tight skin, predictable routines, control over adult children—the more we exhaust ourselves. Adaptation begins with acceptance, not resignation. It's the radical act of saying, "This is happening. Now, who do I want to be in response?"

Second, we get curious. Instead of asking, "Why is this happening to me?" we start asking, "What is this change trying to show me?" Sometimes change is an ending. Sometimes it's a nudge. Sometimes it's a neon billboard screaming, "YOU WERE MADE FOR MORE!"

Third, we build resilience habits, small anchors that help us feel grounded during flux. It could be a morning walk, journalling, a group text with friends who don't flinch at the word "perimenopause," or just five minutes of silence where no one needs anything from you. (Revolutionary, I know.)

By midlife, we've got plenty of habits: It means we keep showing up. Even when our pants don't fit. Even when the dream shifts. Even when we are still figuring it out.

Here's what no one tells you: You've already survived 100% of your worst days. You have faced change before. You've rebuilt, redefined, and risen. Midlife isn't the first time you've adapted. It's just the first time you are doing it unapologetically—and maybe with a better playlist.

Because you, my friend, are not falling apart. You are unfolding.

DISCOVERING NEW VERSIONS OF OURSELVES

There's a sacred moment that comes in midlife, usually when you don't expect it.

Maybe you're standing in the grocery store, staring at 14 brands of almond milk and wondering when life got so complicated. Or maybe you're lying in bed at 2:00 a.m., wide awake for no apparent reason except that your hormones now think they are in charge. And out of nowhere, a quiet voice inside you asks, *Is this it? Is this who I really am?*

It's not a crisis. It is a calling.

Midlife is an invitation to meet ourselves again. Not the version shaped by everyone else's expectations, but the version we've kept tucked away. She's still there. Maybe she got buried under carpools, conference calls, PTA meetings, and meal prep. But she didn't disappear. She just went underground for a while, waiting for you to come back and ask, *What do I want now?*

That question is the starting point of rediscovery. And the answers? Sometimes surprising, often delightful, occasionally terrifying.

You might discover you no longer want to be the glue holding everyone together—and guess what? You don't have to be. You might realize you love watercolor painting, or hiking, or starting a business, or finally learning what TikTok is about (or at least pretending to for your grandchildren). You might decide that quiet mornings, real friendships, and being wholly yourself are worth more than all the gold stars you used to chase.

Some of us find creativity in midlife that we didn't know we had. Others find courage. Or clarity. Or a capacity for joy that's no longer tied to anyone else's approval.

This is the season of reclaiming your voice—and letting it get a little louder. It's when "maybe someday" becomes "why not now?" and "who do I think I am?" turns into "actually, I do know who I am, thank you very much."

Here is the best part: there is no one right version of you to discover. You don't need a rebrand or a makeover. You're not lost; you're unfolding. And every version of you has value—the tender you, the messy you, the daring, daydreaming you, the wise and wildly human you.

This is not a comeback. You are not returning to who you used to be. You are arriving—fully, finally—as the woman you were always becoming. So, ask yourself: What haven't I tried yet, simply because I thought I was too late, too busy or not enough?

Try it. Even awkwardly. Even scared. Because this part of your life isn't about proving yourself. It's about freeing yourself.

You've earned the right to explore, expand, and surprise yourself. This is your permission slip. Signed, sealed, and maybe scented with eucalyptus oil.

HABITS THAT SERVE THE WOMAN YOU'RE BECOMING

Let's talk habits—not the "biting your nails" ones, but the ones that quietly shape your life, one day at a time.

By midlife, we've got plenty of habits: the way we start our mornings (with or without caffeine and existential dread), the way we react when someone pushes our buttons, the way we care for others (and possibly forget to care about ourselves). Many of these patterns were formed long ago, before we were even aware we were making choices.

But now? Now you're not just surviving. You are choosing. And that means it's time to take inventory. Which habits are still serving you—and which are silently sabotaging the woman you are becoming?

Let's start with a truth bomb: Your habits are less about discipline and more about identity. The things you do daily are tiny declarations of what you believe about yourself. Are you someone who prioritizes joy? Rest? Movement? Boundaries? Chocolate before 9 a.m.? (No judgement.)

Too often, we think of habits as one more self-improvement project. One more list to conquer. But at this stage of life, habits aren't about perfection—they're about alignment. They are about creating rhythms that support your peace, your energy, and your worth.

So, what habits feel like worth?

1. The habit of saying no. Without explanation. Without guilt. Without any explanation why it's okay for you to prioritize your time.

2. The habit of checking in with yourself before checking on your phone. (Wild, right?) Even just one minute of breath and intention before diving into the digital world can shift your whole day.

3. The habit of moving your body, not to punish it, but to celebrate it. Dance, stretch, walk, lift, wiggle—it's not about size or speed. It's about joy!

4. The habit of delight. Fresh flowers. A funny podcast. A five-minute stare at the clouds. Midlife gets better when you sprinkle in small sparks of light. . . glimmers.

5. The habit of *not* doing it all. Let the laundry sit. Let someone else plan the thing. Rest is a habit, too—an act of rebellion in a culture that worships hustle.

Changing habits doesn't require a whole personality transplant. Start small. Think tiny hinges that swing big doors. One better choice at a time, anchored in the truth that you are worth the effort—not because you are broken, but because you are becoming.

You don't need to overhaul your life. You just need to create a few new rituals that reflect the woman you are choosing to become—not the one you've outgrown.

So go ahead and light the candle, take the walk, say the "no," pour the lemonade, and choose the habits that whisper, *this is who I am now.*

THE POWER AND POSSIBILITY OF NOW

There comes a point—somewhere between sagging and soaring—when you realize, this is it. This moment. This life. Not the one you planned, the one you curated for Instagram, or the one you thought you'd be living by now.

Just this. And somehow, that's more than enough.

The mirror still catches me off guard some days. I'll catch a glimpse and think, wait. . . when did I become my mother? (And if you were lucky enough to have a good one like mine, maybe that's not such a bad thing, after all.) You may see wrinkles you earned the hard way, laugh lines from the decades you survived, soft edges where sharpness used to be. You will see life.

But now, instead of sighing, you start to smile. Because the woman staring back at you? She knows things. She's weathered storms, lost pieces of herself, loved deeply, lost deeply. And risen anyway. She is not here to shrink or apologize. She is here to shine. Maybe quietly, maybe wildly, but unmistakably.

There is power in midlife, not because everything is figured out, but because you've finally stopped trying to be someone else. You've dropped the need to prove. You've let go of the illusion of perfection. You've learned to choose peace over performance, purpose over people-pleasing, freedom over fear.

Here is the real magic: it's not too late. It never was. The possibility of now is richer than anything that came before, because you get to decide what comes next— with no one else's permission.

Midlife isn't the end of any road. It's the part of the story where the heroine stops trying to be relatable and starts being real. It's where she turns toward the mirror, not to critique, but to say: Thank you. You've carried me this far. . . let's go even further.

So, raise a green smoothie to the woman you're becoming. She is worthy. She is wise. She is wonderful.

And she is just getting started, just like Janet.

> There is power in midlife, not because everything is figured out, but because you've finally stopped trying to be someone else.

Everything that you've experienced in the past is what has made you the person that you are now. . . and I help you to see that person, because this is the space in which I live and grow. Visit my website, book *your free call,* and download my **Midlife Momentum Booklet.** I'll help you begin to:

- Love yourself and your life so you can stop being stuck in the past.
- Engage with your present life and find joy in it.
- Create a beautiful, purpose-filled future.

CHAPTER 6

Self-Care Reimagined: The Radical Act of Choosing Yourself in a World That Taught You Not To

Kelly Arthur

Certified Life Coach & Licensed Therapist

kellyarthurcoaching.com

instagram.com/kelly_arthur_coaching

linkedin.com/in/kellyarthur-9b9b645

Kelly Arthur is a certified life coach and burnout survivor who helps women in midlife reclaim their time, energy, and sense of self—without dropping the ball at work or at home.

With a master's in social work and advanced certification in motherhood and family life, her coaching blends deep clinical expertise with practical tools and insight shaped by real-world experience. Kelly knows what it's like to give until there's nothing left—and how hard it can feel to choose yourself.

She's the creator of *Path to Purpose*, a signature program designed to help women reconnect with themselves and move forward with clarity and intention. Her approach is warm, honest, and built around the belief that you don't have to burn out to make a change— there's a gentler way forward, and it's within reach.

Kelly lives in Massachusetts with her husband and two daughters. These days, her version of self-care looks less like meditating at sunrise and more like pausing to be present—and helping other women do the same.

"You love me, Mommy?"

My three-year-old, snuggled into her pink-footed pajamas, sat cross-legged on the floor in front of me while I typed furiously on my laptop. It was 7 p.m., and I was trying to finish a work email before the nighttime routine chaos began.

"Yes, I do, honey," I answered quickly, not even looking up. "Let me just finish this email."

I glanced up just in time to see her face fall. Her tiny shoulders slumped, her smile disappeared, and, without a word, she walked away.

I wish I could tell you that night was unusual, but it wasn't. Life was about survival back then: too much to do, too many people to please, and no room to breathe. I had a full-time job in a corporate behavioral health organization, two little girls under the age of five, and a brain running at full tilt from the moment I woke up until I fell asleep.

During the day, I was on edge—snapping at coworkers, hiding my frustration in meetings, pretending I was fine. I wasn't. There was a constant pit in my stomach and that familiar, nagging sense that I was failing everyone. I pushed hard at work to get it all done before the second shift at home: dinner, bath, stories, lunches. And guilt. So much guilt.

Does any of this sound familiar? Maybe you've been there, too—pulled in every direction, doing everything for everyone, and still feeling like it's never enough.

I was always giving. Always scanning for what everyone else needed. But resentment was rotting me from the inside out. My "breaks" were massages I had to negotiate like treaty deals. "Me time" meant cabernet and online shopping for things I couldn't afford (hello, Louis Vuitton bag I've never used). Even weekends away—after the mom guilt and over-functioning just to be "allowed" a break—gave me temporary relief, but no lasting peace. I always came back to the same grind, the same pressure, the same question screaming underneath it all: "Is this really all there is?"

And then everything I was holding together cracked wide open—I had a stroke.

> I thought I just needed a better job or more time alone. What I really needed was permission to slow down.

I couldn't read or write. I couldn't even remember my husband's name. When the speech therapist held up flashcards, I stared at them, lost. My brain—once sharp and capable—was scrambled.

And yet, I wasn't angry. What I felt. . . was gratitude. Gratitude to be alive. To be held. To be forced to stop. My body did what I couldn't do for myself—it pulled the emergency brake.

For the first time in years, I could rest. I couldn't multitask anymore, so I did less. I listened to audiobooks. I lay in the backyard and felt the sun on my face. I napped. I made soup. My husband said, "This is your dream, isn't it? Sitting quietly and not talking to anyone."

He wasn't wrong. I began to see how far I'd drifted from myself. How much of myself I had poured into other people's needs. How much of my life had been about tolerating, not living. I thought I just needed a better job or more time alone. What I really needed was permission to slow down.

The stroke didn't create the crisis. It revealed it.

And the same is true for you. You don't need to end up in a hospital bed to reach your breaking point—that moment when you say, "I can't live this way anymore."

Maybe for you it's something quieter. Chronic migraines. Brain fog. Rage that lives just under the surface. A numbness that creeps in during moments that are supposed to feel full of joy. I've worked with women whose breaking point comes in the form of a panic attack in the car, a bottle of wine that disappears too fast, or a fight with her partner that ends in words she can't take back.

If you're reading this and nodding along, I want you to hear this: It's not your fault. You've been taught that taking care of yourself is a luxury—something allowed only after everyone else's needs are met. You've been taught that you have to earn your rest. That choosing yourself is selfish. That if you pause, something—or someone—will fall apart.

So, it's no wonder self-care feels like an impossible task. When you can't find time for it, you assume you're the problem. But you are not the problem. You've just been handed the wrong definition of self-care. The version of self-care you've been sold? It's built on guilt. On perfection. On lies. And it's keeping you stuck in burnout.

Let's break down those lies.

MYTHS OF SELF-CARE

You hear the word "self-care" everywhere. Whole aisles of Target are labeled with it. Instagram's selling it. Google turns up millions of results telling you what to do, how to do it, and, of course, what to buy.

You've been surrounded by messages about self-care. And for good reason. But the version you've been sold? It's missing the mark.

How do you feel when you hear "self-care?" Eye roll? Pressure? Like you're failing at one more thing? You're not off at a retreat.

You're not meditating at sunrise. You're barely finding time to pee. And yet, you're being told to add a wellness routine to your already packed schedule—like that's supposed to fix everything. That's not self-care. That's marketing.

Myth #1: Self-care takes time, energy, or money.

The truth? You don't need to spend anything to take care of yourself. You don't need to put it on a calendar. You don't need to leave your house. Some of the most powerful self-care practices you can do happen in the middle of a messy day—when you pause before saying yes, when you step outside for sixty seconds, when you ask for space and don't apologize for it.

Myth #2: It's either me or them.

You're taught that taking care of yourself takes something away from the people you love. That there's only so much care to go around, and if you take some for you, you're being selfish. But that's not how this works. When you take care of yourself, you expand your capacity. You become more present, more grounded, more available. Not less.

Myth #3: Pinterest has the answer.

You've been told self-care can be found in products and plans. Fancy routines. Bath bombs and gratitude journals. I'm not against any of it—but if your life still feels like too much after the candle burns out and the to-do list is still staring at you, that's not care. That's distraction.

Here's what I've learned about self-care: Google doesn't have the answer. You do.

You don't need to buy a new version of yourself. You need to remember her. The version of you who didn't ask for permission to rest. Who moved through the day without explaining or apologizing. Who trusted what she needed—before the world taught her to override it.

Self-care isn't about doing more. It's about reconnecting to what matters, and unlearning all the noise that says you aren't allowed to.

That's where we go next.

QUICK HITS VERSUS SUSTAINABLE SELF-CARE

So, what is true self-care? It's flexible. It shifts with your day, your mood, your energy level. Getting a massage on one day will feel like pure relief, but on another day it will feel like just another thing to squeeze in.

It's personal—rooted in what truly nourishes you, not what everyone else is doing. And it's internal. It doesn't have to be scheduled, bought, or shared on Instagram to count.

That's the shift. From self-care that looks good. . . to self-care that actually works.

QUICK HIT SELF-CARE:

You're probably familiar with what I call "quick hit self-care:" the massage, the night away, the yoga class, the girls' weekend you spent weeks planning. These things help. They give you a break. A moment to breathe. You feel better—refreshed, even.

But here's the catch: they don't change what you come back to.

The to-do list is still there. The pressure is still buzzing under your skin. Quick hit self-care gives you relief—but not repair. It helps you step back into a life that's still draining you. And before long, the magic wears off.

You need this kind of self-care. It matters. But it's not enough on its own. To feel different in your life, you need both the ease in the moment and the transformation over time.

SUSTAINABLE SELF-CARE:

This is where you start addressing the patterns that created your stress in the first place. If quick hit self-care is a bandaid, sustainable self-care is the cure.

But even when we know these changes matter, we resist them. Why? Because sustainable self-care often means disappointing someone, stepping outside your comfort zone, or risking conflict. It's not easy. But it's how you build a life that feels like yours.

It looks like asking for what you need. Saying no to what drains you. Resting when your body needs it. Asking for help. Setting boundaries. These aren't indulgences—they're long-term solutions that ease stress at the source.

How do you know you're practicing sustainable self-care? It's uncomfortable. It's vulnerable. It's unfamiliar. And then— it's empowering. You feel proud. You notice change. You begin showing up differently in your life.

Let's see it in action:

Meet my client, Jennifer, a 45-year-old corporate lawyer with three school-aged kids, a packed calendar, and a running mental list that never seemed to end.

She'd tried all the "right" self-care—workouts, a watercolor class, a gratitude list, even drawers full of unopened mindfulness books.

In our work together, we focused on bringing in sustainable self-care—starting with naming what she needed and giving herself permission to ask for it.

She wanted more balance in managing the house and kids but feared disrupting the unspoken rules she and her husband had created as a couple. We worked on calming her nervous system, practiced scripts to use with her husband, and focused on what this shift could mean for her family: less stress, more ease, a mom who wasn't constantly running on empty. She started with low-stakes requests—small asks to flex a muscle she was just learning to trust.

At first, she tried: "I'm realizing I've been holding more than I can manage. Can you take the lead on grocery shopping this week?" and built up to asking for more shared responsibility, even when it meant disrupting old patterns.

It felt uncomfortable at first. But with practice, it got easier. The tension at home began to shift—and so did her sense of self. She started speaking up sooner, resting before she hit a wall, and showing up more fully in her life.

This wasn't really about her husband. It was about Jennifer claiming space in her own life—one bold choice at a time.

If your shoulders tense reading that, you're not alone. Asking for what you need can feel risky—especially when you've been taught to avoid disappointing others at all costs. But ask yourself: What's the cost of never asking? Of always ignoring your needs? Of slowly disappearing from your own life?

This is what sustainable self-care really looks like: honest, sometimes uncomfortable, but it's how real change begins. It's not always easy, but it creates space for the life you truly want.

In the next section, I'll walk you through how to build your unique version—one small, consistent step at a time.

YOUR SELF-CARE, YOUR WAY

By now, you've seen how varied real self-care can be—and how possible it can feel. You don't need a ten-step wellness routine or a fridge full of green juice to take care of yourself.

Wondering how to bring this into your own life? I created something for you: the *Unique Self-Care Plan*, a free guide to help you start small, stay consistent, and build a version of self-care that truly works for you. You can download it here: www.kellyarthurcoaching.com/selfcareplan.

Because real self-care can be:

- Sensory: what helps you feel grounded and calm in your body.
- Emotional: what allows you to feel and process.
- Boundaries: what helps you say no or pause.
- Asking/Receiving: what reminds you that it's okay to ask for support.

But where do you begin when there still feels like no time, no energy, and no room for you? There is a way in—and it starts smaller than you think. Let me introduce you to someone who thought she had no time at all.

"Every part of my day belongs to someone else."

That's how Amy described her life when we started working together. As the director of a teen crisis center, Amy handled everything from staffing and budgets to supporting students in emergencies. The days were long, the pressure constant. Amy felt like she was failing everywhere. She couldn't be enough at work or at home. Setting boundaries felt selfish, even cruel. So, she kept absorbing it all.

One night, after a brutal workday, her mom called five times in a row. Amy picked up—knowing it would drain her, but not knowing how not to. The conversation escalated. She hung up on her mom for the first time ever—and then sat in silence as the tears came. Not because of the call, but because she realized how depleted she felt. She wasn't just tired. She was disappearing.

We began with one simple shift. She reclaimed ten quiet minutes each morning for herself—no calls, no emails. She turned off her phone at 9:00 p.m. She stopped answering every time it rang. At work, she delegated instead of doing it all herself. Together, we wrote scripts that helped her respond to her mom with clarity and care, such as , "I know this is hard, but I'm not able to talk right now. I'll check in later this week." Instead of defaulting to yes, she gave herself space: "I'll get back to you."

She practiced setting boundaries—at home, at work, with herself. And slowly, she started to see the difference between what was truly urgent and what was just static.

Of course, the guilt showed up: "I'm a terrible daughter." "What if something happens?" "If I don't handle it, who will?" But she stayed with it. We worked through the resistance. And over time, something shifted.

"I didn't think it was possible to feel like this," she told me. "I finally feel like I have room to breathe. This is a gift."

....

Self-care isn't about adding more to your plate—it's about clearing space for what matters.

....

A SELF-CARE PLAN FOR THE LIFE YOU ARE LIVING NOW

Self-care isn't about adding more to your plate—it's about clearing space for what matters. It starts with listening to what you need and honoring it in ways that feel doable and real. One honest step at a time. And from there, it grows.

This is your invitation to pause and check in—with curiosity, not judgment. Ask yourself:

- What deeply nourishes you—not what looks good on Instagram, but what makes you feel most like yourself?
- What's one thing you used to love but haven't let yourself do in years?
- Where are you saying yes when your body is quietly saying no?

Real self-care might look like:

- Watching true crime in pajamas with zero guilt.
- Sitting in your car for five extra minutes before walking inside.
- Saying, "Let me check my calendar," instead of immediately saying yes.

These aren't luxuries. These are nervous system resets. Small moments that bring you back into your body and back into your life.

Remember Jennifer's story? Here is an example from her life:

- Self-care practice: Sending a meme to my best friend every day at 3 p.m.
- Why it works: It reminds me I'm not alone and makes me laugh.
- When: Mid-afternoon, when I usually hit a wall at work.
- How I'll build it in: I set a recurring reminder on my phone.
- What it creates in my life: A moment of connection, a moment for me that resets my energy.

And yes, resistance will show up. If you think:

80   SHE RISES

- *I don't have time.* Try pairing it with something you already do. Jennifer started with three slow breaths before logging into Zoom. She didn't carve out a new routine—she reclaimed a quiet moment that was already there.

- *This feels uncomfortable.* Jennifer started with a small ask—her partner switching the laundry loads while she wrapped up work. Practicing the request built her confidence for the harder ones ahead.

- *What if someone gets upset?* Discomfort is part of change—but so is relief.

When Jennifer first said no to a last-minute weekend work request, she felt the old urge to over-explain. Instead, she practiced a calm, clear boundary: "I won't be available, but I'll circle back on Monday." The discomfort passed, and she reminded them—through action—that her time matters, too.

You don't need to have it all figured out. You just need one small shift that reminds you: I matter too. That's how it started for Amy—with ten quiet minutes in the morning. That one act of self-care opened the door to more clarity, more boundaries, more space.

Your version of self-care might look different—and it should. Because your life, your needs, your nervous system—it's unique to you.

I still remember the day my youngest sat cross-legged in her pink pajamas, waiting for me to look up from my laptop. I missed it—her face, her need, that moment—because I was trying so hard to keep up. That version of me was exhausted and disconnected.

Now, I pause. I look up. I'm here. And if I can find my way back, you can, too.

Let this be your turning point. Not a dramatic change, but a real one. One step that supports your peace. Then another. And another.

This is your moment. Not later. Not when things calm down. Now.

CHAPTER 7

Inner Boundaries: The Secret to Feeling Happy, Joyous, and Free

Eugenie D. Basu

Master Certified Life Coach

askeugenie.com

As a master certified life coach, Eugenie helps her clients create meaningful, sustainable changes in their lives— both inside and out. Whether your goal is career success, deeper relationships, or personal well-being, she will work with you to identify your key challenges. Often, these obstacles stem from self-management issues and one's relationship with oneself, resulting in stress, burnout, anxiety, self-doubt, resentment, negative thinking, and a persistent sense of feeling stuck or unhappy—even when outer success has been achieved.

With 20+ years of experience as a yoga and meditation instructor, and advanced expertise in healing touch energy therapy and clinical aromatherapy, she brings a deeply holistic lens to coaching. Her background also includes an MBA and an MA in theoretical linguistics, allowing her to blend structure, insight, and intuitive presence. Her clients often say they feel truly seen and heard—able to connect to their own truth and finally make themselves a priority.

Eugenie's coaching integrates emotional intelligence, nervous system awareness, and inquiry-based reflection. Together, she and her clients clarify their goals, explore what's true for them, and strengthen the inner foundation that makes them feel they are living a life they love.

• • •

Have you ever found yourself thinking, "I just need to get through this week"—again? You're doing everything you can. There's a list waiting before your feet even hit the floor: lunches to pack, deadlines to meet, messages to answer. You meant to wake up early and do something just for you—a walk, some quiet, a deep breath. But you went to bed late again, scrolling long past midnight, chasing a sliver of relief that never really came.

On the surface, you're capable, holding it together. Underneath, the tension builds. You snap at your partner for asking a simple question. You feel guilty for how you rushed the kids out the door. And when you finally carve out an hour for yourself, you don't follow your own plan. You clean. You scroll. You avoid getting started. And then you criticize yourself for not using your time "better."

What if the real issue isn't your time, your to-do list, or your willpower—but your inner boundaries? What if the freedom you long for—and the deep feelings of joy and happiness that seem just out of reach—aren't "out there," waiting in the next relationship, achievement, or lifestyle change. . . but already within you, in the form of inner structures either waiting to be remembered, or to be consciously created?

While external boundaries get most of the attention—saying no, setting limits, drawing lines—it's the internal ones where real transformation begins. They shape how you show up in the world. They shape how grounded and resilient you feel when life becomes overwhelming and chaotic—and when you face significant pressure or criticism from the expectations of others. They are the agreements you've made with yourself about what you'll tolerate, what you believe you deserve, how much space you take up, how much of yourself you're allowed to bring forward, and which parts of yourself you must keep hidden.

Without strong internal boundaries, you're likely to bend toward others' expectations and abandon your own needs. You may find yourself saying yes when everything in you says no, staying silent when truth burns in your throat, or slipping into overwork and overgiving—then feeling so off-center, so resentful, so lost, so exhausted, so overwhelmed, so anxious.

But something begins to shift when you consciously "architect" the agreements that govern your time, your truth, your energy, and your worth; you create a deep internal safety. A steadiness. A return to yourself. Because freedom isn't the absence of structure—it's the presence of the right ones.

INNER BOUNDARIES

Unlike outer boundaries, which help manage how others treat you, inner boundaries guide how you treat yourself—especially when you're torn between rest and responsibility, avoidance and action, or your needs and others' expectations. They don't live in theory; they come alive in practice, moment by moment.

A protective inner boundary might sound like: I stop working when I feel depleted. It's a decision to listen to your body and energy, and to honor your well-being instead of overriding it out of habit or guilt. These kinds of boundaries are essential. They act like internal safeguards, helping you say no—not to punish or restrict yourself, but to preserve what matters most.

Some inner boundaries are generative, which means they support something new, healthy, or life-giving. These boundaries help you create space—space to rest, to focus, to grow, to be who you are without apology. A generative boundary might say: I block off Sunday mornings for my writing because it feeds me. Or: I give myself permission to do less when I'm grieving. These boundaries don't just protect you—they nourish you. They help you live more intentionally, from the inside out.

Here are four forms that inner boundaries might take:

- Limits—the clear "nos" that protect your time, energy, or values.
- Commitments—the steady "yeses" that keep you anchored in what matters.
- Permissions—the inner allowances that help you soften harsh self-demands.
- Attunements—the ongoing practice of listening to your internal signals and responding with care. (I listen when my energy shifts.)

Each of these forms offers something different. But all of them help you stay in the right relationship with yourself.

WHY INNER BOUNDARIES OFTEN GO UNNOTICED

Most of us didn't grow up hearing about inner boundaries. We may have been taught how to behave, how to follow rules, or how to treat others—our external boundaries. However, our internal boundaries are invisible and unspoken, yet they shape our thoughts, feelings, and choices in subtle but powerful ways.

From a young age, most of us learn by observing. And if the adults in our lives didn't model strong internal boundaries—like resting when they were tired, saying no without guilt, or tending to their own emotions—then we likely didn't learn how to do those things either. Not because anything is wrong with us—and not even because our caregivers didn't love us—but because they may not have known how to offer that kind of care to themselves either. Our nervous systems learned from theirs, so we don't notice when something inside us feels off—tired, tense, pushed too far, or quietly calling out for attention.

Many of us are still learning how to tend to our feelings. That's part of why inner boundaries can go so unnoticed. They aren't about managing other people's behavior. They're about tending to your own inner life—your feelings, your limits, your truth. And because they're often invisible and rarely named, we don't always recognize when they've been crossed.

Sometimes we don't even realize that we're reacting to an old, unmet need. There are emotional reasons why inner boundaries get buried. Sometimes, when we do notice a boundary—like the need to rest, or the urge to say no—it's accompanied by guilt, fear, or shame. Over time, if those feelings aren't understood or supported, we may start ignoring our boundaries altogether. And yet, these internal agreements are some of the most important ones we'll ever learn to keep.

That's what this chapter is about: beginning to notice, name, and rebuild the inner boundaries that protect your well-being, support your truth, and allow you to live in deeper alignment with yourself.

WHY INNER BOUNDARIES ARE SO HARD TO HOLD ONTO

Even when inner boundaries exist, they are often fragile or underdeveloped. They tend to collapse or crumble under pressure, whether from constant demands at work, unresolved conflicts in close relationships, overwhelming emotional stress, or the exhaustion of caring for others without replenishing yourself. These pressures chip away at your internal limits, leaving you vulnerable and depleted.

Inner boundaries need to be consciously recognized and strengthened to protect your well-being. They don't just fall apart because someone else is harsh or because your energy is low. Often, they weaken for quieter, more complex reasons. You may struggle to maintain these boundaries for many reasons, including:

- You're not clear on what you want or need. No one ever asked you, or if they did, it wasn't safe to answer honestly. Even as adults, your first instinct is to scan for what's expected or acceptable, not for what's true inside.

- You don't feel as if you have permission to prioritize yourself. You may believe your role is to be the "strong one," the "easy one," or the "giver."

- You worry that having needs will threaten the relationship. You might default to "I'll fold so there's no conflict," even if it puts you in conflict with yourself.

- You haven't learned how to stand your ground without shutting down or lashing out. Without guidance or modeling, we often struggle to find a middle ground, swinging between two extremes.

- You don't yet trust that you matter—even to yourself. Reinforcing a boundary takes energy and intention. But when we doubt our worth, we're less likely to use that energy to protect our time, honor our truth, or choose what nourishes us.

- You confuse inner boundaries with control. Instead of focusing on your own internal agreements and self-care, you get caught in trying to manage or change others, believing that if you can "fix" the outside, you'll finally feel safe and whole inside.

Before moving on, it's helpful to check in with yourself. Do any of these patterns feel familiar? Which one speaks to you most right now?

WALKING THE TIGHTROPE: CHOOSING YOURSELF WITHOUT FEAR

One of my clients was worried about something that carried a lot of weight for her: she was dreading telling her current hairdresser that she was switching to someone else. She had found a neighbor who cut hair at home for a fraction of the price and who could easily fit her into her schedule. It was a clear, practical choice. Yet, inside, she felt like she was walking a tightrope—torn between taking care of herself and the fear of upsetting her stylist.

When she shared this with me, our conversation went something like this:

Client: "I just don't know how to tell her. I'm afraid she'll be hurt or angry. She's really counting on me, and I feel guilty like I'm letting her down."

Me: "It sounds like you're caught between your own needs and this worry about how she'll react. That's a tough place to be."

Client: "Yes, exactly. I know I need to do what's best for me—especially with my budget and time—but I feel so stuck. I feel torn, like I'm walking a tightrope. I want to respect her, but I also need to protect my energy and finances."

Me: "And you absolutely can do both. Can you give yourself permission to choose yourself here, telling her your decision without needing to justify or explain it beyond what feels right for you?"

Client: "I guess I can, but I'm afraid of how she'll take it. I don't want to make her upset or angry."

Me: "It's natural to feel that way, especially when you care about someone. But remember, it's not your responsibility to control or fix her reaction. Her feelings are hers to take care of. Maybe she will be upset when you tell her you are switching to another stylist. In that case, can you let it be okay that she has feelings about it?"

Client: "I would feel so responsible. And like I'm a bad person or did something wrong."

Me: "Are you a bad person for letting her know your decision? Is that really true?

Client: "No, now that you ask me, it's not really true. I just feel so conflicted about it."

Me: "I understand. What if you can just let this feeling be for now, let it be okay, without trying to push it away because it is so horrible? That feeling does not have to stop you. You can decide to be on your own side. And you can still speak respectfully and kindly when telling her about your decision. Your responsibility is to be honest with yourself and act in integrity with your own needs."

Hearing her story, you may relate. Maybe you've felt that same inner tug—wanting to set a boundary, but being held back by fear, guilt, or the struggle to put yourself first. This story shows how inner boundaries protect you and give you permission to live in alignment with your truth, even when it's hard.

WHAT HAPPENS WHEN YOU DON'T PROTECT YOUR OWN NEEDS

Let me share another story. A client came to me recently, feeling completely overwhelmed. She was a working mother trying to balance the constant stream of needs pulling her in different directions. What she needed was time—solid, uninterrupted blocks of time to do her work—but no matter how much she told herself she'd carve that time out, it never happened. She'd make a plan in her head, but when the time came, she wasn't rested, couldn't focus, or found herself pulled in ten other directions.

She felt guilty taking time for herself when her family needed her. Even when the space opened up, she was too tired to use it well, or she'd fill it with something else that felt urgent in the moment. And when she did finally sit down to work, she'd find herself scrolling, stalling, distracted. She'd beat herself up for procrastinating, for not using the time well, and feel like she was letting everyone down—her clients, her kids, herself.

Eventually she'd snap—yelling at her kids for interrupting, even though she hadn't actually set any clear boundary around her work time. She hadn't told them what she needed. She hadn't blocked the time off on her calendar. She hadn't set herself up to succeed.

When she described this to me, I could hear how much she was blaming herself. But what was actually happening wasn't a failure of discipline or motivation—it was a lack of internal structure. Her inner boundaries weren't holding. She hadn't given herself permission to take her work seriously. She hadn't set limits around her time. And she hadn't accrued the resources—physically or emotionally—to be able to do the kind of deep, focused work she needed to do.

As we talked, we looked at the patterns together: how often she overrode her own needs, how rarely she claimed time without guilt, how frequently she kept going even when she was exhausted. We began to identify what was missing—not just outer boundaries with her kids or her schedule, but inner boundaries that gave her permission to rest, to protect her energy, to prioritize what matters.

That's where we started: not with a perfectly color-coded calendar, but by helping her connect to the part of herself that knows she's allowed to matter, that her time is worth protecting. We explored how she could support herself on purpose—anticipating the moments when she'd need focus and preparing for them. That meant setting limits around bedtime the night before, blocking off work hours in a visible way, and feeling good when she took time for herself. These weren't just productivity tweaks. They were acts of self-trust. As she practiced these new boundaries, things began to shift. Her focus improved, her patience grew, and her self-talk started to soften. She began to meet herself with more grace, and in doing so, reclaimed energy that had been lost to guilt and shame.

For her, moving ahead meant learning to say:

- "I need focused time for my work."
- "It's okay to take rest the day before so I can show up fully."
- "I'm allowed to prioritize my needs without guilt."

Then, setting these boundaries leveraged several clear, practical steps:

- Blocking out work hours visibly on her calendar, so her family could see and respect that time.
- Establishing signals with her kids—like a closed door or a timer to create predictable focus periods.
- Creating a routine for rest and winding down the night before to improve energy.
- Practicing self-compassion, gently catching negative self-talk, and reminding herself that rest and focus are necessary, not optional.

These intentional practices weren't about forcing perfection or creating rigid schedules. They were about creating structures that support her well-being, so she could meet her responsibilities without losing herself in the process.

As she practiced these boundaries, she began to notice a shift—not just in what she accomplished, but in how she felt about herself. The constant tension eased, patience returned, and the cycle of guilt started to break. Most importantly, she was learning to treat her own needs as important—not optional—and that changed everything.

WHERE FREEDOM BEGINS

Inner boundaries aren't built in one big decision. They're built in small ones—moment by moment, choice by choice, decision by decision. Every time you pause before saying yes. . . every time you notice your own need instead of rushing to meet someone else's. . . every time you bring your attention back to yourself, you are building.

At first, it takes effort. You may feel uncertain or clumsy. But with practice, these choices begin to take root. They become felt experiences—not just ideas, but truths you live. Over time, they internalize. They become natural. They become you. Life—which once felt unmanageable, stretched thin, or ruled by other people's needs—begins to open to you, not through one sweeping change, but through many small, faithful acts of self-honoring. You find more ease. More clarity. More peace.

This is how you return home to yourself. Not all at once, but through the power of consistency. Each boundary you build is a step back to that steady, whole, free place inside.

This is where freedom begins—inside you, with you, as you. Building inner boundaries isn't about creating walls or rules that restrict you. It's about creating a strong, loving foundation within yourself—a place where you can return again and again, no matter what life throws your way, so you can truly be happy, joyous, and free.

Each moment you pause to check in, each choice you make to honor your needs, and each boundary you set adds strength to that foundation. Over time, these intentional practices become second nature. They shape a life filled with greater ease, joy, and peace. Remember, this is a journey, not a one-time fix. Freedom begins here—in the small, daily acts of coming home to yourself.

If you're ready to take a small step toward building boundaries with support or find out more about how we can work together to help you live a life that feels truly yours, please visit my website askeugenie.com.

CHAPTER 8

When the Soul Whispers "Enough": Heeding the Quiet Voice That Calls for Rest, Not Perfection

Sondra Sperry

Holistic Master Certified Coach

🌐 coachwithsondra.com

f facebook.com/sondra.sperry

📷 instagram.com/sondrasperry

Sondra Sperry is a trauma-informed, holistic master certified coach who creates deeply safe and ethical spaces for women to reconnect with themselves, release perfectionism, and return to peace. With a background in transformational coaching and decades of lived experience, Sondra helps women soften the noise of hustle culture and hear their own inner wisdom again.

She guides clients through burnout, self-doubt, and overwhelm with steady compassion—inviting them to pause, breathe, and rebuild trust in themselves. Her coaching is grounded, heart-centered, and rooted in the belief that we are already enough.

Sondra lives in Utah, where she enjoys slow mornings, time in nature, meaningful conversations, and every opportunity to connect with her three children, their spouses, and her six grandchildren.

"I don't love you anymore."

My head was spinning. I felt nauseous. It was as if my life was crashing down around me. Have you ever felt like everything you were holding together suddenly came undone? Like you were doing everything you knew how to do—and it still wasn't enough? You're not alone.

My husband and I had three young children—a three-year-old, a six-year-old, and an eight-year-old. I was doing my best to be a good wife, to create a loving, comfortable family life. I was trying to hold everything together. But in all that striving, I didn't see what it was doing to us.

He didn't feel needed. I had taken on everything—carrying the weight, managing the details—and unintentionally left no space for him to belong. He couldn't name exactly what was wrong. He just knew something felt off.

At the time, I didn't understand. I thought if I just did more, tried harder, was better, everything would be okay. But we were both lost in roles and expectations that left little room for real connection. And I didn't yet know how to hear my own voice, let alone hold space for his.

Just before my 29th birthday, he said it—those words that shook my world: *"I don't love you anymore."*

I couldn't stop crying. I tried to hold it together, but I was unraveling. I prayed—desperately. I even prayed it was somehow my fault, because if it was, maybe I could fix it.

We met with our spiritual leader. He reminded us of our covenants and urged us to try—for the children. He arranged counseling.

The first counselor was terrible. My husband refused to go back. My sister recommended someone else. That counselor said he wouldn't meet with my husband unless he called to set it up. He wasn't going to waste time with someone who didn't want to be there.

So I went alone. He told me that one day, I'd come to a session and not be crying. I didn't believe him. But eventually, it happened. And that was the beginning of my healing. It was the first time I heard, "You don't have to do more." The first time I felt a whisper in my soul: *"Enough."*

You are good enough. You are doing enough. In fact, you may be doing too much. You don't have to be perfect. And perfection, I learned, doesn't make people love you more.

Do you relate to this? Do you try so hard to do things perfectly that you're not even sure how you feel anymore? Do you find yourself exhausted from trying to make everyone else happy—only to realize it's not working for them, and it's definitely not working for you?

You're not alone. It's natural to want those you love to be happy. It can even feel easier to be okay when they're content. Sometimes, it can seem like your happiness depends on theirs.

But when you begin sacrificing your own needs, constantly managing others' emotions, comparing yourself, or tying your worth to perfection, it's easy to lose yourself. When you can't rest unless everyone else is okay, it's a sign. It's time to pause, to re-evaluate. To find a different way.

One woman I worked with was a devoted mother with a full-time job, an elderly parent who relied on her, and extended family who often turned to her for help. She loved keeping an organized home and wanted to be there for the people she loved, but she was exhausted.

She told me how hard it was to say no. If there was time on her calendar—even if she didn't want to spend it that way—she felt obligated. "If I can do it, I should do it," she said.

Her grown children were frustrated by how much time she spent caring for her father. Her marriage was strained. Emotionally, she felt stretched far too thin. She carried an invisible weight—the belief that she was responsible not just for her father's care, but his emotional well-being too. Like many women, she had been abandoning her own needs to keep the peace.

In our sessions, we began gently shifting that pattern. Through mindful journaling and tender self-inquiry, we created a sense of safety in her body—a place she could return to without judgment. She started checking in with herself more regularly, noticing her needs, and meeting them with compassion.

Slowly, things began to shift. The weight didn't vanish overnight, but with intentional practice, she began to feel it lift. One day, she said, "It feels so freeing to be able to speak up and say 'no' from a loving space."

That's what happens when you begin turning inward, not to disconnect from others, but to reconnect with yourself. You stop abandoning your own needs in the name of being "good." You realize love doesn't require exhaustion. And you begin to reclaim your right to rest, to choose, and to be whole.

What if it doesn't have to be so hard? What if joy doesn't have to come with pressure, stress, and comparison? What if it could be simpler? What if joy could return—not by managing everyone else's emotions, but by coming home to yourself? Not in a way that pushes others away, but one that grounds you in clarity and connection.

This path came from my very soul. It's a journey I've walked for years. It didn't happen overnight, but I've come through it, and I now know: it's a path worth exploring.

As I write this, I'm honestly in awe of how far I've come. The version of me from years ago couldn't have shared any of this. I would've worried too much about how it would be received, what others would think. It would've felt too vulnerable. Too exposed. But healing softens fear and makes space for a calm reassurance that didn't exist before.

When I was 49, my husband passed away. That loss—on top of everything I'd already walked through—became the catalyst for the most significant transformation of my life.

Shortly before he passed, my daughter introduced me to coaching. I had already begun healing, but I was still stuck in old patterns of striving. Coaching shifted everything. I became a life coach. I dove into thought work. It was powerful. For the first time, I had tools to examine my thoughts, challenge old beliefs, and consciously choose something new. But even then, I realized that I couldn't think my way through everything.

I was still pushing. Still forcing progress. My nervous system was overloaded. I was deeply exhausted, and mindset work alone couldn't fix that. I wanted to build my coaching business—truly wanted it—but I couldn't force myself to make it happen. No matter how hard I tried, I couldn't push through. My mind was flooded with judgment over all the things I wasn't doing. I felt like I was failing. Eventually, I realized I wasn't lazy or broken—I was overloaded. My nervous system was trying to protect me the only way it knew how: by slowing me down.

That was a turning point. I began tending to my nervous system with gentleness instead of force. I started rewriting the quiet stories running in the background of my mind—the ones that said I had to earn love, prove my worth, manage other people's emotions, and stay small to keep the peace. As I healed, I began to believe something radical: I am not responsible for other people's feelings. I don't have to be perfect. I am good enough as I am.

As those truths took root, something unexpected happened: I could show up without feeling sick inside. I didn't want to cancel or hide. One day, during a group conversation, I shared openly. For the first time in a long while, I didn't second-guess myself afterward. No shame spiral. No overanalyzing. I simply spoke—and it was okay. That moment revealed how far I'd come.

I had lived with the constant chatter in my brain for so long, I didn't even realize it was there until it was gone. I thought it was just who I was. I didn't know peace like this was even possible.

When I began coaching other women, I saw that I wasn't alone. The stories varied, but the deeper truth was the same: They were all mired down by quiet exhaustion, fear of not being enough, the heavy weight of over-responsibility and perfectionism.

Now, my work is about helping women soften those same patterns—not by pushing harder, but by honoring their bodies, their stories, and their worth. The tools that changed my life are the very ones I now offer. I work with women who've spent years trying to be everything to everyone—good wives, mothers, daughters, employees—yet still feel like they're falling short. I can hear it in their voices: the weight of striving, the ache of "not being enough." I recognize the signs—not because I have all the answers, but because I've lived it.

One client spent her life trying to feel "good enough" for a parent who struggled with severe mental illness. As a child, she took on the impossible task of managing her father's emotional world—always trying to be perfect, say the right things, avoid setting anything off. Over time, she came to believe her worth depended on keeping the peace.

In our sessions, we slowly gave voice to that younger version of her—the one who had carried so much responsibility that was never hers to hold. We honored her pain. We made space for her truth. And then, something shifted. One day, she said, "It wasn't about me, was it?"

That moment changed everything. She finally saw that her father's reactions weren't a reflection of her worth. They were his story—not hers. The shame she had carried for decades began to soften, replaced by a quiet, deep-rooted self-compassion.

As I continued listening to women's stories, a pattern became clear: so many of us are taught to work harder when things don't feel right. To fix. To carry more. To be better. But that only drives us further from ourselves.

So I want to say this clearly: You are not failing. You are responding exactly the way in which you were conditioned. But there is another way—a quieter, more honest way. A way that begins, not with doing more, but with pausing.

I've walked this path. I've watched others walk it. And while each journey is unique, the turning point is always the same. It begins with a whisper: You don't have to keep proving your worth. You are already enough.

Maybe you're still feeling unsure. Maybe you've spent so long on autopilot, or living to meet others' needs, that you're not even sure what you need anymore. Maybe you've forgotten how to listen to yourself—or maybe no one ever taught you how.

LISTENING INWARD

Here's something you can try today: Place your hands gently over your heart. Close your eyes. Take a slow, deep breath. As you inhale, consciously soften. Let your shoulders drop. Invite the muscles in your chest and belly to relax. Imagine your breath creating space around your heart—space for stillness, presence, and listening.

Then, in a tender inner voice, ask:

"Sweet girl, how are you doing today?"
"What do you need from me right now?"
"How can I love you a little better at this moment?"

And then. . . just listen.

If what comes up is a long to-do list, gently ask: "Do I really need more to do right now?"

And if the answer is yes: "What's one or two simple things I can do to support myself?"

What if you trusted that less is more? What if simplifying—letting go of the noise—is actually the path to the peace you crave?

Try this practice first thing in the morning, then again when you feel overwhelmed or anxious. The more you return to this space, the more clearly you'll see what you truly need. This is how you begin to know yourself. This is how you rebuild trust with your inner voice.

You are not alone. If you're tired, it's not because you're weak. If you're overwhelmed, it's not because you're doing life wrong. You've likely been doing the best you can in a world that constantly demands more—more effort, more perfection, more proving.

But what if more isn't the answer? What if the healing you long for begins with one small breath of permission: "You're allowed to rest." You don't have to earn your worth. You don't have to keep proving yourself. You're allowed to slow down. To change. To choose a new way forward—one that honors who you truly are and the life you long to live.

WHAT IS REST?

The kind of rest I'm talking about isn't just a nap or vacation—it's a soul-level exhale. A homecoming to yourself. It's what happens when you stop performing, stop proving, and stop pushing past your limits. It's the quiet confidence that you are enough, even when you're not doing anything at all. It's the freedom to pause, to feel, to know that your worth isn't tied to your output.

This is where healing begins—not by doing more, but by allowing yourself to just be.

Rest is how you speak to yourself. It's how you let imperfection exist. It's how you breathe in the present moment. It's not what happens when you're done. It's what makes you whole while you live.

LOOKING BACK

I wish I could go back and whisper to the woman I once was. Here's what I wish she knew—what I want you to know, too.

For a long time, I lived from the outside in. I measured my worth by how well I kept up, how happy everyone else was, how much I got done. I believed that if I could just be good enough, helpful enough, loving enough—then I'd finally feel peace.

But peace doesn't come from proving yourself. It comes from knowing yourself. And that begins when you learn to listen inward.

THREE TRUTHS THAT CHANGED EVERYTHING

1. **Doing more isn't always better.**

    We live in a culture that glorifies hustle. But healing doesn't live in hustle, it lives in the quiet moments of your life. Sometimes, the most courageous thing you can do is pause. When you slow down, you can finally hear your own voice again—the one that knows what matters and what you're meant for.

One client shared, "Through our work, I stopped chasing perfection and started learning how to love myself where I am. The shift from self-criticism to self-acceptance changed everything—including how I show up in my work and life."

That's what this work makes possible.

2. **You are not responsible for everything.**

   If you care deeply, it's easy to carry the emotions of others, but their happiness isn't your responsibility. Your peace doesn't depend on keeping everyone else comfortable. You're allowed to let go. You're allowed to stop carrying what was never yours to begin with.

   > **Sometimes, the most courageous thing you can do is pause.**

   One woman I worked with said, "Coaching helped me move through a painful situation with more peace and clarity. Instead of spiraling, I learned to pause, reflect, and actually grow—which deepened my relationship with myself and those around me."

   That's the power of letting go of control and choosing growth instead.

3. **Trusting yourself is sacred work.**

   Rebuilding trust with yourself—especially after years of outsourcing your worth—is tender and brave. It may feel uncomfortable at first. But the more you listen to your intuition, the more she'll speak. The more you honor your boundaries, your energy, and your needs, the more solid and grounded you'll become. This isn't selfish. It's sacred.

   One long-time client said, "Each session helped me see my progress through a more compassionate lens. I started noticing my wins instead of discounting them—and that small shift began rebuilding my confidence in a lasting way."

   That's what coaching is meant to be: a safe place to remember your strength and rebuild belief in yourself.

ONE LAST WORD BEFORE YOU GO

If this chapter stirred something in you—if you felt seen, or even just a little curious—it might mean a part of you is ready to breathe deeper, to let go of the pressure, and come home to yourself. That readiness is enough.

> Rest isn't what happens when you're done. It's what makes you whole while you live.

I want you to know: healing is possible. Peace is possible. You don't have to wait for a crisis to begin listening to that small, sacred voice inside you whispering, *"Enough."* Enough striving. Enough performing. You are already enough.

Though this may be the only chapter you read from me in this book, I want to leave you with something to carry with you. If you feel ready, I've created a free set of journaling prompts to help you begin tuning into your inner voice—gently, honestly, and with love.

To download your companion guide: *Coming Home to Yourself*

Scan the QR code or visit:

☞ https://www.coachwithsondra.com/journal

These prompts are a beginning. A quiet invitation to sit with yourself in stillness and hear the wisdom that's always been there. Let them meet you where you are. No rush. No pressure. Just presence.

This is your beginning. You are not broken. You are becoming. Let this be your sacred pause. Your quiet moment. The beginning of your own *"enough."*

As you move forward, I want to leave you with a blessing—a gentle reminder for the journey ahead:

May you trust the quiet moments.
May you give yourself grace in the in-between.
May you feel the solid ground of your enough-ness.
May you rest.
May you rise.
May you come home to yourself.

Rest isn't what happens when you're done. It's what makes you whole while you live.

CHAPTER 9

What the Brain Needs to Heal, and the Body Longs to Feel: Restore Regulation and Joy with EFT Tapping and Breathwork

Marianne Brereton

Clinical EFT Practitioner and Breathwork Facilitator

mbeftandbreathwork.com

instagram.com/mariannebreretoncoaching

facebook.com/marianne.brereton.2025

linkedin.com/in/marianne-brereton

Marianne Brereton is a certified clinical EFT practitioner and breathwork facilitator. She is a health and master certified life coach, and is certified in advanced motherhood and family life.

Her passion and purpose are helping other women gently release stored emotions, regulate their nervous systems, and reconnect with who they were always meant to be. After her own journey through the trauma of early childhood abuse, self-abandonment, and chronic stress, she discovered that true healing begins not in the mind, but in the body.

Today, she guides women with deep compassion—offering a safe space for discovery, growth and transformation.

Marianne is a lifelong learner and lover of books, as well as the beauty of nature, especially cool mountain air, fragrant pine trees, and watching sunsets at the beach.

She has been married to the love of her life for over 50 years and treasures time with her children, grandchildren, and her two golden retrievers, who are never far from her side.

For more information about Marianne and the evidence based, scientifically studied gentle and softening techniques that she uses to bring the women she serves the regulation and truth they are searching for, go to her website at: https://mbeftandbreathwork.com/.

W hat if I told you that much of the pain that you experience emotionally and physically may be caused by the emotions trapped inside of you? What if feeling your emotions—and finding safety in your nervous system's responses—could shift the beliefs and patterns that hold you back? What if that shift could open the door to your dreams and allow joy to return, even amid challenges?

For most of my life, I was the silent one—holding everything together for everyone else while quietly unraveling inside. I didn't know that what I was experiencing was difficulty regulating my nervous system and stored trauma, and that I'd developed a habit of self-abandonment. Like so many women, I thought healing meant fixing myself by being more productive, more focused, more everything, and doing it alone. What I needed was safety to feel, release, and reconnect—to remember who I was before the world told me who to be. Somehow, I needed to reconnect with the parts of me that were disconnected to survive the pain of the past. How, though?

As a little girl, I thought my life was pure magic. . . just like I considered my grandparents' beautiful garden to be, where I spent my days dreaming about a fairytale world filled with all the beauty that I so desperately desired. I was always dreaming, and everyone thought that I was a shy, quiet child. I had no reason to believe any differently without knowing the hidden truth.

For many years, my negative memories were no worse than occasional nightmares and strange dreams of hidden monsters in the closet or under my bed—that would be normal for most any child. Then my fears gradually started becoming more real. The older I got, the more I realized that something was not right in the version of the past that I remembered, and that there were many gaps that didn't make sense. There was always conflict and confusion within me that was difficult to understand. I couldn't remember ever doing anything bad; I always tried to be a good girl and never caused any trouble. But the nightmares persisted, and I held it all inside.

As humans, we all have amazing and beautifully created brains, complete with a complex nervous system that is programmed to protect us from the things that we might not be able to handle, especially when they happen at a very young age. My brain did its job well, but my body was holding onto more suppressed emotions than it could bear. Eventually, the effects of long-held hidden memories, beliefs, and patterns formed by those early years began to rise to the surface.

When I eventually realized what had been done to me at such a young age, the confusion made more sense—and so did the hurt and lack of trust. The person I had trusted completely and looked to for safety and protection was the one who had abused me and hurt me more than anyone else in my life for many years. He then lied and said it was only curiosity. Violation and physical harm are not just curiosity.

> Your healing begins the moment you feel safe again.

The past control I thought I had of my mind, body, and heart was shattered, and nothing seemed real. In an instant, everything was different. I was terrified of what could happen next. I trusted no one. Fear became my normal, my constant companion, and my greatest struggle. Generalized anxiety and panic were my labels, and, for a time, defined me. I felt damaged in a way that I thought I could never fix.

Healing can begin at any time and in any season of life, and the only requirement is a willingness to take a chance on yourself and to be open to what may be the best, most challenging, and beautiful ride of your life. Your healing begins the moment you feel safe again.

Healing is a mysterious process that is so individualized, with many twists and turns, as it's impossible to foresee what lies ahead. It is never linear, nor is it in any way predictable; it is often cyclical and the things you may feel in one way today could be felt differently tomorrow. The emotions that you think are gone now may return next week in a completely different context, always presenting possibilities and opportunities that you may have never imagined.

This journey may appear as a long road, beginning with finding what is possible and effective to heal whatever your challenges are, and then discovering the best path and guidance to help that will allow you to feel completely safe and comfortable reaching for something that, at this time, may not seem fully possible.

Taking care of yourself and your needs may feel as foreign to you as it did to me. It went against everything I had believed for most of my life. I thought that serving others somehow was not only my purpose but my salvation in life, and that my value and worth were based on my actions, not my existence. I loved being a wife and mother, but had no connection with myself, and had little understanding of how important that was in finding the "me" that had been shoved deeper into darkness.

After becoming a certified health and life coach, I realized that although cognitive coaching was my first step toward uncovering myself again and getting in touch with my thoughts, something was still missing, and that something was needed so much more. I began the process of finding that missing piece when I became interested in becoming trauma informed, and a whole unfamiliar world emerged. Finding emotion work and Clinical EFT (tapping) led to me coming home to myself and unlocking the parts of me that I had hidden and forgotten for over six decades.

I rediscovered EFT, or Emotional Freedom Techniques, which I had studied years earlier. My first experience with tapping had been fifteen years prior, when just basic EFT existed, with nine simple techniques, which consisted of gently tapping on acupressure points with the fingertips while thinking and saying statements about the problem. This would send a calming signal to the body and brain.

For those of you reading this chapter who have little or no understanding of EFT tapping, please watch this short video that explains what it is, how it works and why:
https://mbeftandbreathwork.com/tapping-video/.

In the early stages, EFT lacked the hundreds of scientific studies that have now been done to show the evidence of its effectiveness. That's where the difference lies between basic and clinical EFT. It has now also expanded to forty-eight techniques and is used on everything from stress to phobias, insomnia, anxiety, PTSD, and more. The latest studies—one of them a 2025 meta-analysis now published in the prestigious *European Archives of Psychiatry and Clinical Neuroscience*—reveal that EFT outperformed virtually every intervention it was compared against for treating PTSD.

Emotions are a gift that we all have been given. They are messengers, and when you turn towards them with curiosity, not judgement, things begin to soften.

When you cry, it isn't just an emotion, it's also biological. Tears help you to release a stress hormone called cortisol that gently allows for that release. As you release cortisol, you also create calm in your body. Crying also activates your parasympathetic nervous system—the "rest and restore" part—which slows your heart rate and deepens breathing. Your brilliant body knows exactly how to regulate your nervous system if you listen to it. Honoring the importance of your body's innate ability to regulate and create safety is a fundamental right, just as breathing 22,000+ times a day is essential to survival.

When I began working with my own clinical EFT practitioner, I found the gentle, understanding soul who I needed most. She was introduced to me earlier through another program and I knew that her personality, her empathy and experience with the techniques were what I needed to feel safe and able to trust her fully. As she became a witness to my pain, validating all that it meant to me, it allowed me, week by week, to ease into healing and processing both in body and mind.

Not only that, but the more I learned about myself and what was true for me based on my values and my worth, the greater the light I felt inside me, and the more joy I experienced no matter what I faced. With time, I became more and more comfortable being in my own body and understanding how to work with my own emotions.

That's what led me to become a certified clinical EFT practitioner, and later a functional breathwork facilitator. When I discovered the benefits of breathwork and how well the two worked together, I knew that I had to incorporate both into my work.

Breathing is a necessary part of life, but most of us have never learned how to use our breathing in the most effective ways. Dysregulated breathing is so common in most people, and they have no idea how little it takes to calm the mind and regulate the nervous system with simple breathing practices. When someone tells you to breathe, do you breathe through your mouth and lift your shoulders with tension, or do you relax your shoulders and breathe with your mouth closed through your nose? Breathing not only affects your nervous system, but every system in the body, and it changes the level of energy you can access.

My work helps women like you regulate their nervous system, build their resilience, and gently release long suppressed emotions, as they thoughtfully rebuild their lives from the inside out. Through a blend of evidence-based and studied EFT techniques and guided breathing practices, I create safe spaces where women can explore the truth of their experiences—without shame, without rush, and without judgment from others.

One of my long-term clients, who we will call Grace, came to me with some deep, traumatic memories, including an experience that happened to her six years ago involving her beloved motorcycle. This had changed her ability to enjoy something that she previously loved. She now was limited by her fear and unsurety of her own ability.

While riding with her husband, still getting used to her new Harley-Davidson on a curvy stretch of road, she made a split-second decision to try and keep up with him and, as she came into a curve too fast, she suddenly stopped trusting herself. She crossed into the oncoming lane, rode into a wet ditch, and hit a tree. She walked away and the bike was fixable, but she still carried the invisible injuries, the fear, the guilt, and the anxiety. It returned in full force every time she tried to ride again.

As we worked through her memories and her emotions, using a technique called "Tell the Story," she was able to not only remember the things that had happened during the accident, and the intense feelings that came up during our sessions together, but also many things that she had forgotten that made the entire story take on a different meaning. Each time something felt activating to her and she could feel the fear or the anxiety, we stopped, and she was able to spend time working through each emotion, tapping on the acupressure points until it no longer brought any of those old feelings. This technique is often used when there are a series of events that can be recalled. When used with trauma, it is done very slowly and carefully so that no details are missed that could come up later.

I was amazed as I witnessed her transformation and her ability to access the thinking and decision-making part of her brain, the prefrontal cortex, which I refer to as the "CEO." When we are in fight or flight, we do not have access to this decision-making area of the brain. Tapping through the entire story, she was able to get past the fear and lack of confidence that had accompanied the accident and had lingered for so long. She became able to ride that same motorcycle again without hesitation.

I had the honor and ability to guide her through the technique and help her work through all that came up, but she was the one that courageously faced her fears and did all the work needed to heal and find safety once again.

In the moment of witnessing such beautiful shifts in perspective and change in understanding with a cognitive reframing, I am often filled with feelings of deep gratitude and love. The glow that comes in those "aha!" moments can be beyond explanation.

When a client who has lived stuck in fight, flight, or freeze mode gradually shifts to a rest and recovery state of calm and relaxation, it is something that is immediately visible. Often, they will start yawning and feel very sleepy, and some not only feel calm, but are also energized. Everyone's body reacts differently; some need a lot of time to process the changes and others have an immediate response.

I have always loved working with clients that have never experienced tapping, or those who have never even heard of EFT. It is especially satisfying to see those who respond very quickly once they are taught how to tap on the acupressure points, and when they use even the most basic techniques to alleviate pain, stress, or even sadness. Whether it's a lack of understanding or doubt that anything so simple could work, it is equally a pleasure to see the excitement in their faces as they realize that something is happening and that their discomfort or suffering is finally softening or going away.

I had a wonderful session with a client who I will call Tessa, while she was experiencing a great deal of sadness in her whole body due to grief and loss. She was grieving her husband, who she loves deeply. He is still in her life, but for only a short time, due to early onset Alzheimer's. Some days, the weight of that reality is so hard for her to bear. I asked her if she wanted to try a basic tapping round where we simply used our fingers to tap on the nine acupressure points on the face and upper body, and as we did it together, she focused on her feelings of sadness and overwhelm.

Before we could even finish with one round of tapping, she stopped to ask me what I did and how I did it. The truth was I had done nothing but teach her a beautiful method of releasing her unfelt emotions that were coming out in ways that were causing stress, overwhelm, and confusion. She was so responsive that she began feeling better instantly as we continued tapping together.

During my year and a half of certification and mentoring in Clinical EFT, I worked with many women who were struggling with chronic stress, anxiety, grief, PTSD, shame, insomnia, chronic fatigue, trauma, depression, lack of self-worth, phobias, addictions, and so much more. I found that no matter what the situation was or what emotions came up, if you have a place of safety and where you are seen and heard, it is possible to heal with time and the willingness to feel what has been held inside. The changes that come and the joy that emerges along the way are worth all the work. Part of the idea for my business came from asking one simple question: "What if we gave ourselves the same care and compassion we give to everyone else?"

I now offer group programs, one-on-one coaching, and guided practices that invite women to carve out even just one hour a week to breathe, to feel, and to discover their truth. . . because healing doesn't require suffering or a loss of self—it just requires a willingness to begin, taking one step at a time.

Go to this link to experience your own EFT and breathwork practice: https://mbeftandbreathwork.com/journey-of-discovery/.

Every woman deserves to feel like herself again.

This work has become my passion and purpose in life. It lights me up every time I meet with women who are searching for answers and brings me so much satisfaction, not for what I have accomplished, but for the miracles I see in other women every day.

You don't have to hold it all together anymore.

You've carried so much for so long—pain that wasn't yours to bear, expectations that silenced your truth, and patterns that kept you small just to feel safe. Confusion that makes your nervous system stay dysregulated. A lack of awareness that could help you to find the freedom that comes with regulation.

You don't have to be fixed.

Now, you can choose yourself.

You can choose safety.

You can choose gentleness instead of survival.

You can reclaim the parts of you that you lost to fear.

You get to become the woman you were always meant to be: whole, valued, and worthy.

Your healing doesn't have to look anything like anyone else's.

So, take a deep slow breath.

Place your hands over your heart. Close your eyes. Again, one more time, breathe. . . deep and slow.

Remember: You don't have to be fixed. It is never too late. . . Your time is now, and you don't have to rush. Read that again!

And this time, you don't have to do it alone.

Many women struggle with chronic anxiety, stress, and physical pain that conventional healing can't fix. You can use EFT tapping and breathwork to rewire your nervous system so you can experience more joy and feel like yourself again.

CHAPTER 10

Perfectly Disguised: Behind The Mask Of Having It All Together

Angela Gaskin

Master Coach

angelagaskincoaching.com

facebook.com/profile.php?id=61561552352875

Angela Gaskin is a master certified life coach, speaker, and founder of Life Built Right Coaching, where she helps women build emotional resilience and create meaningful, lasting change. Drawing from her own journey through heartbreak, healing, and reinvention, Angela blends deep empathy with practical, science-backed tools to guide women back to their authentic selves.

Her coaching philosophy is rooted in the belief that true strength comes not from perfection, but from the courage to be vulnerable and real. She empowers women to release the pressure to perform, reconnect with their faith, and rediscover their worth from the inside out. Through intentional self-connection, mindset work, and tools like Emotional Freedom Techniques (EFT), she helps her clients cultivate inner safety and confidence from within.

Whether speaking on stage or coaching one-on-one, Angela continues to inspire women to live authentically, rise from life's most difficult moments, and step boldly into their true power.

From the outside, no one would guess. Your hair is curled, your smile polished, your calendar color-coded. You're the woman others whisper about in admiration: "She's amazing. I don't know how she does it all."

But behind the curated confidence and Instagram-worthy snapshots, you're a woman barely holding it together. You cry in the shower where no one will hear. You volunteer for one more thing to avoid the silence at home. You smile through gritted teeth while resentment brews just beneath the surface. You are the go-to friend. The dependable wife. The tireless mom. And you are exhausted.

What others don't see are the late nights spent replaying conversations, wondering if you said the wrong thing. They don't hear the voice whispering, "you're not enough," no matter how much you do. So, you carry on. Perfectly disguised. Hiding behind a mask of having it all together. Until the cracks grow too wide to hide.

This was me. . . but I didn't even know I was wearing a mask, because it was all I had ever known. One day, sitting in church, I heard a well-meaning call to serve more, give more, be more. Everything in me wanted to show up. But I had nothing left. I was drained. Depleted in every way.

I thought I just needed a break. A long time out.

At the time, I was working full-time, raising kids, managing business finances, serving at church, juggling sports, groceries, laundry—all the things. And I held myself to impossibly high standards. I wore the mask of excellence like a second skin. But underneath? I was crumbling.

It didn't make sense. I had survived worse: two divorces, juggling work and college while navigating single motherhood. I had since remarried a wonderful man and was raising a blended family of seven amazing kids. Life looked full and inspiring. And yet, I was more miserable than ever. The guilt piled on top of the exhaustion. I kept thinking: Other people do more. I've handled worse. Why can't I keep up?

The truth? My body and soul were sounding an alarm. This time, there was no pushing through. However, slowing down felt like failure. Like I was letting people down. Like proof that I wasn't enough. This is the story so many women silently live.

WHY WE WEAR THE MASK

No one puts on a mask without a reason. We don't wake up one day and decide to hide who we are—we do it because, at some point, it feels *safer* to do so. Safer to be polished than real. Safer to stay quiet than risk being misunderstood. Safer to be who others needed us to be than to ask what *we* needed.

These masks form slowly, often without us realizing it. They help us avoid pain, rejection, or vulnerability. They keep us functioning, showing up, and meeting expectations, even when we're crumbling inside. But, over time, what once felt like protection starts to become a prison. We begin to lose touch with our own voice, needs, and truth.

Here are some of the most common reasons women disguise themselves behind the mask of "having it all together"—and why it makes so much sense, even if it's silently exhausting.

1. To Avoid Judgment

   You fear being seen as weak or too much, so you tone yourself down to be accepted.

2. <u>To Earn Worth Through Performance</u>

    You've learned that what you do equals who you are. Productivity becomes proof of value.

3. <u>To Keep the Peace</u>

    You suppress your emotions to avoid conflict. You smile and serve while resentment simmers.

4. <u>To Maintain Control</u>

    You micromanage, overachieve, or people-please not because you're confident, but because you're afraid of what might happen if you're not enough.

5. <u>To Avoid Facing the Deeper Pain</u>

    Busyness and perfectionism distract from the grief, fear, or loneliness buried beneath.

But here's the truth: The mask may protect you, but it also *disconnects* you. It keeps you from intimacy, authenticity, and peace. Worst of all, it convinces you that you must keep performing to be loved.

You don't.

WAYS THESE MASKS SHOW UP IN REAL LIFE

These emotional masks often become so familiar, we don't even realize we're wearing them. They show up in the small moments: in how we show up for others, how we avoid our emotions, and how we try to prove our worth.

Here are three of the most common masks women wear—and what's really hiding underneath.

<u>Mask of Perfectionism:</u> *Always polished and productive, avoids failure, never asks for help.*

- The mom who bakes homemade snacks, volunteers at every school event, and keeps a spotless home—but cries in the shower because she feels like she's never enough.

- The successful businesswoman who's constantly pushing herself for the next promotion—while silently battling burnout and imposter syndrome.

- The woman in church who gives powerful talks, leads every committee, and never shares that her marriage is falling apart and her kids are falling away.

What's behind it? A belief that "if I do everything perfectly, I'll finally be enough—or at least no one will see how unworthy I feel underneath."

This was evident in a client I will call Gloria. Behind closed doors, she was struggling. She often lost her patience, snapped at her kids, and then felt crushed with guilt. She wanted to be the calm, loving, supportive mom—but some days, it felt impossible.

Deep down, she was terrified that her emotions meant she was failing. *If I were a good mom, I wouldn't feel this way,* she thought. Everyone else seemed to have it figured out, but she was exhausted, overwhelmed, and silently drowning in mom guilt. Admitting she was struggling felt like admitting she wasn't enough. . .

<u>Mask of People-Pleasing:</u> *Always saying yes, avoiding conflict, prioritizing others' needs while neglecting your own.*

- The friend who's always available, even when she's exhausted— afraid that saying "no" will make others stop liking her.

- The daughter who agrees with her parents' expectations out of fear of disappointing them—even though it's not the life she wants.

- The coworker who takes on extra work to avoid conflict with the team, then quietly resents everyone.

What's behind it? A fear of rejection, abandonment, or disapproval—and the belief that love must be earned through sacrifice.

This was true for Liz. She wore her "I've got it all covered" mask like armor. She was the dependable one. The helper. The one everyone could count on.

She picked up extra shifts, came in on her days off, canceled her own plans to say yes to others—all in the name of being helpful. From the outside, she looked like the ideal employee: reliable, selfless, passionate. But behind the polished mask, she was quietly falling apart.

Liz was running on fumes. Every time she said "yes," a part of her whispered, *what about me?* But she brushed it aside, afraid that saying "no" would make her seem selfish or weak. Somewhere along the way, she had confused love and responsibility with self-sacrifice.

Underneath it all was a fear she rarely admitted out loud: *"If I don't hold it all together, everything will fall apart—and it'll be my fault."*

Mask of Buffering: *Overeating, overworking, over-scrolling to avoid discomfort.*

- The woman who comes home from work, brings out the ice cream, and numbs out with Netflix instead of facing her loneliness.
- The high achiever who fills every spare moment with to-do lists so she doesn't have to sit still and feel sadness or grief.
- The mom who snacks all day or scrolls endlessly just to escape the overwhelm she doesn't know how to name.

What's behind it? Discomfort with difficult emotions like shame, fear, sadness, or insecurity, and a subconscious belief that "feeling is unsafe."

That was my story.

After I discovered coaching, I began to uncover the ways I was buffering with busyness. I filled every moment with a task: cleaning, organizing, managing the household, showing up for the kids. Even in downtime, I stayed busy, always doing, never just being.

And when I finally paused—even for a moment—I'd reach for food. Overeating became my secret escape from the chaos I had created. It was my quick hit of comfort. A moment where I didn't have to perform or *feel*—I could just escape.

I thought I just needed a break. But the truth was, I was hiding deep insecurity: the fear that if I stopped proving my worth through productivity, people would see I wasn't enough. That I'd be exposed as a failure. I had mistaken performance for value and control for safety. So even though my life was full, it left me feeling empty, and depleted.

HOW TO REMOVE YOUR MASK

Wearing a mask can feel like second nature. We get so used to pretending we're okay, we forget what it feels like to *actually be* okay. But behind every mask is a woman who's longing to breathe. To be seen. To stop performing and finally just *be*.

Removing the mask doesn't mean exposing everything all at once. It means taking gentle, courageous steps toward being more honest with yourself and others, without shame, without pressure.

Here's how to begin: Not with force, but with compassion. Not by proving anything, but by reclaiming who you really are, one small step at a time.

STEP 1: NAME THE MASK YOU'RE WEARING

Ask yourself: *"Where am I pretending to be okay when I'm not?"* This step is about becoming *honest and curious,* not critical. It's gently noticing where you might be performing instead of showing up as your true self.

What this could look like:

- You show up to the school event with a big smile—even though you cried in the car.
  - *Mask of Strength or Perfectionism:* "If I look strong, I won't feel weak."
- You say "yes" to watching your niece again, even though you're overwhelmed.
  - *Mask of People-Pleasing:* "If I say no, they'll think I'm selfish."
- You scroll on your phone for an hour instead of journaling like you meant to.
  - *Mask of Buffering:* "It's easier to distract than to feel."

By naming the mask, you take the first step toward removing it. Not to shame yourself, but to make space for what's real. Because you don't need a mask to be loved. You just need to be *you.*

STEP 2: PRACTICE SAFE SELF-EXPRESSION

Ask yourself: *"Can I be just 2% more honest or real right now?"* You don't have to bare your soul or rip off the mask all at once. Just take one small, brave step toward authenticity.

What this could look like:

- Instead of saying "I'm fine," you say, "It's been a hard day, actually."
  - *Replying honestly without oversharing—just enough to be real.*

- You tell your spouse, "I could use a little extra support this week."
  - *Asking for help in a low-risk way.*
- You let yourself cry in front of a friend instead of brushing it off with a joke.
  - *Letting emotion be seen, even just for a moment.*
- You cancel a plan with kindness instead of pushing through your burnout.
  - *Honoring your limits and being honest about your capacity.*

Start with one person, moment, or sentence. **The goal isn't to be radically vulnerable, it's to be** *gently real.* Because when you practice small acts of honesty, you begin to build trust with yourself and others—and that's how true connection grows.

STEP 3: SURROUND YOURSELF WITH SAFE, HONEST COMMUNITY

"You don't have to do this alone."

> The goal isn't to be radically vulnerable, it's to be *gently real.*

Healing doesn't happen in isolation. It happens in connection—with people who let you be messy, real, and in-process. When you're used to wearing a mask, being truly seen can feel scary. But with the right people, it can also feel like relief.

Here's what this might look like:

- You text a trusted friend, "Can I be honest? Today was hard." And instead of fixing it, she just listens and says, "Me too."
- You join a small group or support circle where people are open about their struggles. You realize you're not the only one trying to hold it all together.

- You meet with a coach or therapist who reminds you that you don't have to earn your worth with perfection—that being human is more than enough.

- You start slowly sharing more of your truth with people who have earned the right to hear it—not everyone, just the safe few.

STEP 4: USE EFT (TAPPING) TO CREATE INNER SAFETY

We often hide behind masks because something deep within us doesn't feel safe being fully seen. Whether it's fear of judgment, failure, shame, or the need for control—our nervous system will block vulnerability if it senses danger. That's why *lasting change isn't about willpower—it's about safety.* This is where Emotional Freedom Techniques (EFT)—also known as *tapping*—can be a game changer.

What is Tapping?

Tapping is a simple, evidence-based technique that combines gentle tapping on acupressure points with spoken affirmations. It's like emotional acupuncture—without the needles. You tap on specific points on your face and upper body while tuning into a difficult emotion, memory, or belief.

> Lasting change isn't about willpower—it's about safety.

The Science Behind It

- *Lowers Cortisol:* A 2012 study published in *Journal of Nervous and Mental Disease* found that a single EFT session reduced cortisol (the stress hormone) by up to 43%, significantly more than traditional talk therapy.

- *Regulates the Amygdala:* The amygdala is the part of your brain that sounds the alarm when it senses threat. Tapping sends a calming signal that helps your brain and body say, "you're safe."

- *Rewires Emotional Triggers:* EFT has been shown to change how the brain associates emotions with certain memories, reducing the intensity of anxiety, fear, and shame.

Why It Works for Mask Removal

You can't be real or vulnerable if your body feels unsafe. This is why you hide.

Tapping helps you:

- Calm the anxiety that comes with taking off the mask.
- Release old beliefs that say you have to perform to be loved.
- Create space for truth, peace, and authentic self-expression.

What This Could Look Like in Real Life

Let's say you're struggling with perfectionism. You might start by tapping on the acupuncture points and saying:

- *"Even though I feel like I have to be strong and have it all together, I choose to love and accept myself."*

- *"Even though I'm afraid people won't love the real me, I'm open to believing I'm enough as I am."*

EFT is powerful because it speaks directly to the part of you that's afraid—not with logic, but with *safety.* And when you feel safe, you no longer need the mask.

Real-Life Examples

Emily, a working mom, was drowning in guilt and overwhelm. She believed, *If I don't do it all, I'm failing.* Through tapping, she repeated: "Even though I feel like I have to hold everything together, I give myself permission to pause." She cried. Her shoulders softened. That night, she asked for help—something she hadn't done in years.

Michael was heartbroken over his daughter's choices but numbed himself with busyness. In our session, we tapped on, *Even though I feel powerless and afraid, I'm open to trusting God's timing.* By the end, he said: "It's still hard. . . but I feel a peace I haven't felt in a long time."

Tanya, a speaker and coach, felt anxious before every talk. Her hidden belief was, *If they see the real me, they won't respect me.* We tapped, saying, "Even though I'm afraid of being judged, I choose to feel safe showing up as me." After a few rounds, her breath deepened. She gave her next talk more grounded and calm.

Removing your mask isn't about perfection—it's about taking small, compassionate steps toward living authentically. Whether you start by naming the mask you're wearing, practicing self-expression, surrounding yourself with a safe community, or using EFT, each step is progress. You don't have to do it all at once.

For more ways to start removing your mask—at your own pace—I've created a free resource to support you. Inside, you'll find even more simple, practical tools you can begin using today, including a beginner-friendly tapping guide, journal prompts, and helpful tips to peel back the layers—one step at a time.

You can access it here: freeguide.angelagaskincoaching.com.

THE STRENGTH BENEATH THE MASK

You were never meant to be perfect. You were meant to be whole: human, messy, growing, and gloriously real. The masks you've worn—whether to appear strong, capable, kind, or unbothered—may have once protected you. But they are not who you are. They've only hidden the beauty of what's underneath: a woman with a tender heart, a resilient spirit, and untapped courage.

Through my own journey of embracing these tools, I discovered that finding myself wasn't just about dropping the to-do list or taking a sabbatical. It was about releasing the belief that I had to *earn* love or *prove* my worth through doing, fixing, or controlling. About creating safety and trust within myself. It meant allowing myself to just be human. Not perfect. Just real.

Healing doesn't mean you never struggle again. It means you finally feel safe enough to stop hiding. To let yourself feel. To let yourself be seen. To tell the truth, even when it's messy. To take off the mask and say, "This is me. And I'm still worthy of love."

So here's the invitation I offer you now:

Slow down. Tune in. Take off the mask, not all at once, but gently, layer by layer. Because underneath the busyness, the buffering, and the pressure to hold it all together. . . is the real you. And she is enough.

Your strength was never in the mask—it's in your willingness to take it off.

CHAPTER 11

Joyful Reinvention:
The Joy of Coming Home
to Yourself

Maria Hendershot

Master Coach

🌐 joyfulreinvention.com

📷 instagram.com/mariahendershot.coaching

Maria Hendershot is a joy revivalist for burned-out moms who are tired of just surviving and ready to create a life with which they're truly obsessed. A master certified life coach with over a decade of experience, Maria holds certifications in life coaching, health coaching, and habit change from The Masterful Coach Collective, The Life Coach School, Tiny Habits, and Faster Way to Fat Loss, among others.

Through her signature "90-Day Joyful Reinvention Program," Maria helps moms identify their energy gaps and make sustainable shifts in mindset, habits, and nervous system health. Her clients go from drowning in to-do lists to living intentionally, feeling like themselves again, and building a life they genuinely love.

A former homeschooling mom of six—now a grandma!—Maria leads by example. After healing from her own burnout, she made a bold move, selling her home to travel the world and reclaim her sense of freedom and joy. She's passionate about helping women feel good enough to dream again, and bold enough to live it out. She also loves dancing, adventures, and crossing items off her wildly imaginative bucket list.

L et me guess.

You're tired. Maybe even exhausted. But not the kind of tired a good night's sleep can fix. You're soul-tired—the kind that comes from carrying too much for too long. You care deeply, you try hard, and yet you still wonder if it's ever enough.

Maybe you're juggling more roles than you can count: mother, partner, daughter, friend, employee, caretaker. And still, it feels like you're falling short somewhere.

I remember once watching an acrobatics performance where women spun dozens of plates on long poles while gracefully dancing across the stage. One even bent all the way backward to pick up a flower without letting a single plate fall. The crowd applauded. It was beautiful. It was mesmerizing. It was. . . familiar.

As I sat there watching, something clicked. *This is me*, I thought. *This is my life.* I'd become a master plate spinner, too, holding everything together: work, family, emotions, expectations. Always running from one thing to the next, determined not to let anything drop. I even got praised for how well I managed it all. But inside, I was exhausted.

Eventually, I reached a point where I didn't want to keep all the plates spinning. Not because I didn't care, but because I craved something else. I didn't want to drop everything; I just wanted to choose differently. I longed to set a few things down, hold one plate at a time with presence, and to just breathe.

That was the beginning of my joyful reinvention, and maybe it can be the beginning of yours, too.

Maybe your days blur into a rhythm of doing, giving, and holding everything together. Even in the rare quiet moments, true rest feels elusive. So you pick up your phone, you scroll, you sigh. And somewhere deep inside, you feel it:

There has to be more than this.

More than pushing through, living on autopilot. More than waiting for the kids to grow up, the house to be clean, or the to-do list to finally be done before you get to feel good.

What you're craving isn't just relief. It's something deeper. It's joy. I'm not talking about the curated kind you see online—not the forced cheerfulness or the pretending everything is fine when it isn't, but real joy. The kind that feels like a deep breath. The kind that feels like *you*.

If you've forgotten what that even feels like, take heart. You're not broken, and you're certainly not alone. This chapter is for you. It's for the woman who's strong and capable, but secretly weary. The woman who longs to feel more alive, grounded, and whole, but isn't sure where to begin. And it's for the woman who's ready to stop waiting and start remembering the joy she was born to experience.

Joy isn't something you have to earn, it's something you reclaim. Joyful reinvention isn't about becoming someone else, it's about becoming more fully yourself and remembering who you were before the world told you who to be.

Let's begin.

JOY REDEFINED

We live in a culture that glorifies hustle and performance while whispering that happiness will come once everything is in place: the clean kitchen, the organized calendar, the cooperative kids. We chase joy like a finish line, only to watch it vanish when life gets messy.

We often think of joy as being the big firework moments: the events, celebrations, vacations, and awards. This leaves us feeling empty in the ordinary moments that aren't Pinterest- or Instagram-worthy.

Joy is often used interchangeably with happiness, fun, or short-term pleasures like chocolate, shopping, Netflix binges, or endless scrolling. These offer relief, but not lasting nourishment. While joy can be found in all of that, joy itself runs deeper. Where happiness is fleeting and circumstantial, joy is enduring and internal. It's an inner steadiness, a quiet current beneath life's surface. It's still there when the dishes pile up and the to-do list goes untouched. Joy is being centered and alive, not because life is perfect, but because you're aligned with what matters, even in the mess.

Joy is always available, you just need to know how to find it. Here are four truths about joy that have shaped both my life and the lives of countless women I've coached.

1. JOY ISN'T EARNED, IT'S REMEMBERED

Maybe you grew up believing joy is something you get after the work is done. You've been taught that feeling good without earning it is selfish or frivolous. Like play and wonder, joy gets sidelined in favor of productivity and responsibility.

But joy isn't indulgent, it's life-affirming. Toddlers don't question their right to enjoy a bubble or puddle. They don't ask if they deserve joy, they simply receive it. You started that way, too, until responsibilities, expectations, and survival mode crowded out your natural access to it.

For many of the women I coach, joy feels like a luxury they can't afford and will never earn. But here's the truth: joy was never external. It's part of who you are, your birthright. You don't need permission, you just need to begin noticing it again. Listen for it. Reclaim it.

Joy doesn't ignore pain or responsibility; it creates space for compassion, presence, and intention. It softens and refills you so you can show up with grace, courage, and abundance, not depletion.

2. JOY IS A PRACTICE

Just because joy is innate doesn't mean it happens passively. Joy is a practice. It's not something that waits for perfect conditions. It's something you learn to notice, allow in, and return to, especially in the ordinary moments. For some, joy lives in creativity. For others, it's found in stillness, nature, or laughter. For many, it arrives with gratitude for the simple things. What matters is that it's true for you.

Joy often finds me in moments of awareness. When I lived on the East Coast during some of the hardest years of my life—nursing babies, homeschooling kids, and navigating grief and burnout—I truly felt like I was drowning. But joy still arrived in small ways: in fiery leaves against a crisp October sky or streets lined with tunnels of pink spring blossoms. Later, after moving to the desert, those seasonal joys were no longer mine to claim. But new joys found me, like vivid sunsets and what I call the "Arizona hug," that moment when the sun wraps around you in a full-body embrace—before you retreat back to the AC, of course! These weren't grand gestures. They were quiet reminders I was still here, and beauty still existed. Every time I chose to notice them, I strengthened the muscle of joy.

Lara experienced something similar. A devoted mom and successful professional, she constantly felt like she was failing in both roles. Life felt like a treadmill—always moving, never arriving. When we began working together, Lara realized she hadn't asked herself what she truly needed in years. So she began practicing small shifts: practicing daily check-ins, giving herself permission to rest, and speaking to herself with kindness. Joy didn't flood in all at once, but it returned in tiny, powerful ways: a solo walk, a spontaneous laugh, a full night's sleep without guilt. With each moment, she wasn't becoming someone new, she was practicing being herself again.

This is the power of noticing. You don't need to chase joy, just make space for it. Every time you pause, breathe, and pay attention, you're practicing. These small moments build a life where joy doesn't have to be earned, just received.

3. THE PARADOX OF JOY

One of the most liberating truths is that joy doesn't require the absence of pain. Joy can sit beside sorrow, and it can coexist with grief, uncertainty, and exhaustion.

Some of the most profound joy I've witnessed, both personally and with the women I coach, emerged in the middle of messy, tender seasons. Even in times of uncertainty, where loss left a hollow space and burnout stripped life of its color, joy still showed up—not as a denial of pain, but as a quiet, steady companion. That fierce, stubborn hope refused to go out, choosing instead to stay and lift.

Joy doesn't cancel pain, but it can soften it. Joy reminds us that even in the darkest chapters, light can still filter in, that you can cry and laugh in the same breath, and that there's space in your life for "both. . . and," not just "either. . . or."

True joy is the fulfillment of experiencing all that life offers: the pleasant and the unpleasant, the delight and the heartbreak. It's the umbrella that stretches wide over the full spectrum of human emotion and says, "I'm alive and I'm living fully."

Waiting for hard times to end before feeling joy keeps us stuck. But when you let joy meet you where you are, it becomes your ally, not because things are easy, but because they're real.

4. JOY BEGINS IN ALIGNMENT AND BECOMES OUR COMPASS

Joy flows most naturally when you're living in alignment with not just your values or passions, but your whole self. This includes your thoughts, your body, your nervous system, your needs, and your desires. It's not about everything being perfect on the outside, but about being honest with yourself deep inside.

Maybe you're doing everything you're "supposed" to do, yet still feel numb or overwhelmed. That's not failure, it's misalignment. Your system (body, mind, spirit) is asking for a reset—not a dramatic overhaul, but a reconnection with what makes you feel most like yourself.

Even small shifts give joy a place to land. Over time, those moments when you feel more whole begin to guide you. Joy becomes your compass, gently pointing you toward what's real and nudging you back to center.

WHERE JOY GETS LOST

If you're reading this and thinking, *but I don't even know what joy feels like anymore,* you're not alone. One of the most common things I hear from women, especially moms, is that they feel this quiet ache for something more. Not for more to do, but to feel more alive.

So what's stealing our joy? I call them *joy zappers*—subtle, sneaky forces that drain our energy and dim our spark. Here are the four most common ones I see:

1. EMOTIONAL DISCONNECTION

When you spend years tending to everyone else's needs, it's easy to lose touch with your own. You stop asking, "What do I want?" or "How do I feel?" because no one else is asking, either. Eventually, you become a stranger to yourself. Your joy didn't disappear; it just got buried.

Imagine a family where one child never gets a turn to pick the game or dessert. When she speaks, she's hushed or ignored. Eventually, she stops asking and tunes out. That's what happens when your needs go unacknowledged for too long. You get the message that you don't matter. Like that child, you slowly check out.

2. COMPARISON

Perhaps you can relate to Kate. She came to me overwhelmed, discouraged, and tangled up in comparison. No matter what she did, it never felt like enough—at least, not compared to her best friend, the woman she silently held up as the gold standard of motherhood, marriage, and success. To Kate, reaching the point where she was just like her friend would mean she'd finally arrived.

One day, I asked, "What if you're not meant to be like her?"

She blinked. "Well. . . I hope that's not true."

"If you spend your life trying to be like her, you'll never have time to be Kate," I replied.

Something shifted. She realized joy wasn't waiting at the end of someone else's story. It was quietly waiting in her own life if she was brave enough to live it.

Here's the truth: You will always fail when you try to be someone else. You weren't made to be anybody but you—the most real, authentic version of you. And the world needs that version. That's a space no one else can fill.

Comparison doesn't just steal joy, it suffocates it. Joy can't grow when you're pretending, it needs authenticity. It takes root when you stop chasing someone else's "enough" and begin honoring what's real for you.

3. CHRONIC OVER-FUNCTIONING

Busy has become the default. Exhaustion is worn like a badge of honor, as is the belief that if you just do more, push harder, or stay ahead, you'll finally feel okay. But hustling your way out of burnout never works. When your nervous system is always on edge, joy isn't just hard to find, it's physiologically out of reach. You're running, not resting. Managing, not living.

I've worked with women who were stuck in over-functioning mode for so long, they didn't even realize they were burned out. One client told me she didn't know how to live without being on edge. Her nervous system was always bracing, always scanning for what might go wrong or what more she should be doing. Rest felt unfamiliar, even unsafe. If she wasn't doing something, she assumed something was wrong.

This is what chronic over-functioning does: it teaches us that stillness is a threat and that productivity is the only way to measure worth. But survival isn't the same as living and it's definitely not the same as joy.

4. AUTOPILOT LIVING

Clarisse was doing everything she thought she wanted—work she enjoyed, raising her kids with love—but still felt empty. When we traced it back, she realized she'd forgotten why she was doing any of it. The rhythm of her days had become so habitual that even the good parts had lost meaning. Once she reconnected with her purpose, even the mundane tasks took on new light. Joy didn't require her to change her whole life, it simply asked her to remember what mattered most.

Autopilot isn't all bad. In fact, it's part of how our brains are wired to help us survive. Automating daily tasks conserves energy and creates efficiency. It's what allows you to brush your teeth while thinking about your grocery list or drive to work without analyzing every turn. It's a brilliant system. . . at least, until it runs the whole show.

The problem isn't autopilot itself. It's staying there for so long that you forget why you're doing what you're doing in the first place.

When life becomes one long checklist, it's easy to lose the thread of meaning. You go through the motions of laundry, lunches, meetings, and bedtime routines, without pausing to ask whether these rhythms still serve you.

Are the habits that fill your days aligned with your values? Do they reflect what matters most to you? If so, wonderful; keep them! Let that clarity renew your energy and motivation, even in the mundane.

But if some of those actions no longer feel necessary and meaningful, you have the power to choose again. You don't have to stay on the hamster wheel just because it's familiar. You can shift from motion without meaning to intention with purpose. Joy doesn't come from doing more, it comes from remembering why you're doing it and doing it with presence, clarity, and heart.

THE PATH BACK TO JOY

It's okay if this feels heavy. The good news is that you don't have to stay here. The way back to joy is simpler and softer than you might think. Joy doesn't require a dramatic overhaul or perfection. It begins with something quieter: awareness. Before you can reclaim joy, you have to reconnect with yourself—what you feel, what you need, and what you want.

Then comes compassion. This is where you meet your thoughts with kindness instead of criticism. It's self-love in action—not just feeling good about yourself, but speaking to yourself with kindness and understanding.

Finally, joy calls you into movement—not frantic fixing, but steady, aligned action. Small, intentional choices that reflect who you are and what matters.

Joy isn't something you wait for, it's something you return to, again and again, with every pause, every breath, every choice to come back to yourself.

If you're not sure where to begin, I've created a free resource called the "Joy Audit"—a simple, powerful tool to help you notice what's draining you and rediscover what's quietly calling you back to life. You can download it at www.joyfulreinvention.com.

Now, let me leave you with this:

I know what it's like to be deep in the thick of it, facing endless to-do lists, piles everywhere, and the hum of constant overwhelm. I know what it feels like to give endlessly while losing your spark. I've lived there.

I can tell you this: one day, the noise will quiet and the lists will shrink. When that moment comes, you might look around and realize you don't recognize the woman you've become, or remember what she loves, dreams of, or what lights her up.

Joy doesn't wait for things to settle, and life doesn't pause until you're ready. What if "later" is now? What if this messy, beautiful season is the one for which you're meant to be awake? So take a moment. Schedule it, if you must. Pour some tea. Breathe deeply. Let the world soften just enough to hear your voice. And, with your hand to your heart, ask, *What do I need right now? What do I really want?* Then honor that truth. Not all at once. Just a little at a time. Because life will keep moving, whether or not you choose to move with it. Let today be the day you choose presence over perfection. Let today be the day you breathe in joy, even when it's wrapped in chaos.

Joy isn't a reward for getting everything right. It's already here, quietly woven into your life. You don't need to become someone new. This isn't about fixing. It's about removing what's in the way of being who you've always been.

Joy begins with one pause, one honest question, one brave, gentle step. Every time you choose it on purpose, you come home to yourself.

This is your joyful reinvention.

CHAPTER 12

From Burnout to Purpose: Redefining Success from the Inside Out

Midore Takada

Master Certified Coach | Holistic & Trauma-Informed
Life Coach | Advanced Certification in Motherhood
& Family Life Coaching

🌐 midoretakada.com

📷 instagram.com/midore_takada_coaching

f facebook.com/midore.takada

Midore Takada is a master certified life coach who helps high-achieving women in midlife step out of burnout and into a life that feels aligned, intentional, and truly their own. Having spent over 25 years in architecture before becoming a coach, she understands the relentless pressure to perform, produce, and hold it all together, all while quietly wondering, *Is this really the life I want?*

Her coaching blends a holistic, trauma-informed approach with mindset work, nervous system regulation, and practical strategies to help women reconnect with their energy, values, and voice without abandoning their ambition. She holds an advanced certification in motherhood and family life coaching and brings deep insight into self-connection, time-energy awareness, and the emotional patterns that keep women stuck.

Midore is originally from Japan, and, after spending 26 years in the hustle and bustle of New York City, she is now based in Richmond, VA. She brings warmth, clarity, and lived experience to every session. Her clients often say they feel "calm, seen, and finally at home with themselves." She meets women at the edge of their next chapter—with a grounded belief that lasting success starts from within.

• • •

B urnout rarely arrives with fanfare. More often, it creeps in quietly—disguised as fatigue, low motivation, or just "too much on your plate." If you're a high-achieving woman, it's easy to dismiss the signs. You might tell yourself it's just a busy season. That if you were more organized, more disciplined, more efficient, things would feel better. Maybe you've told yourself a weekend away would fix everything.

But burnout isn't just being tired. It's being depleted—mentally, emotionally, and physically. Looking back, you may wonder, *Why didn't I see this coming?*

Because burnout builds slowly. Chronic stress piles up, quietly unraveling your capacity over time. And if you're used to being capable and high-functioning, the signs are especially easy to misread. Instead of recognizing emotional exhaustion or disconnection, you blame yourself. Push harder. Try to solve the problem with more effort—when what you truly need is rest, reflection, and reconnection.

Cultural and social conditioning don't help. Think of the praise we receive for staying late, skipping lunch, or bouncing back after a loss. These subtle signals reinforce the idea that rest equals weakness. In so many workplaces—and even within families—productivity is tied to worth. And when you start believing that, admitting burnout can feel dangerously close to failure.

So you power through. You go numb. You silence your internal alarms because the show must go on.

By the time you realize something's wrong, you're already on auto-pilot.

THE HIDDEN COST OF HIGH ACHIEVEMENT

After earning my master's in architecture, I moved to New York City. I'd entered the field later in life and believed I had to work twice as hard to catch up. My younger peers were just starting out, while others my age were already well established. The same "age gap" insecurities I'd wrestled with in school resurfaced the moment I stepped into the professional world.

Still, I was driven. I showed up. I earned my place.

Eventually, I landed a leadership role—with the title, the salary, the team. By every external measure, I had made it. But inside, something felt off. I was stretched thin. Constantly behind. Chasing something I couldn't quite name.

The hours got longer. My body got louder. And no matter how much I achieved, I couldn't shake the sense that I was still falling short.

Maybe you've felt that, too—that quiet disconnect between what your life looks like and how it actually feels to live it.

I started asking myself, softly, at first, "Is this really the life I want?"

WHEN THE ACHE BECOMES TOO LOUD TO IGNORE

It wasn't a dramatic breakdown. No rock bottom. Just a persistent ache I couldn't push away anymore.

The question kept surfacing in the quiet in-betweens. On the subway ride home. In a downward-facing dog yoga position after a long, stressful day. Lying awake at night, replaying conversations during which I hadn't fully been present.

I was efficient, productive—and emotionally flatlining. The joy I once felt from designing beautiful spaces had been replaced by relentless pressure. There was no room to breathe, let alone reflect. I wasn't just tired. I was out of alignment with myself.

But I didn't know how to stop. Or even if I wanted to. I had spent years building a life that looked stable, comfortable, successful. I didn't want to throw it all away. I just wanted to feel like me again—more alive, more connected, more fulfilled.

If you've ever felt that quiet longing—when something feels off but you can't quite name it—you're not alone. You aren't broken. Or lazy. Or ungrateful. You're burned out.

burnout doesn't always look like falling apart. More often, it looks like holding everything together at all costs.

And for women like you and me, burnout doesn't always look like falling apart. More often, it looks like holding everything together at all costs.

THE COST OF UNFINISHED DREAMS

Have you ever quietly let go of a goal that once mattered deeply? Not because it stopped being important, but because life got too full, too heavy, too demanding? Maybe you told yourself it wasn't the right time. Or that it didn't really matter anymore. Maybe you tucked it away and kept going, convincing yourself it was for the best.

I did that, too.

For years, something quietly haunted me. I hadn't finished passing the Architect Registration Exams (ARE)—a grueling series of six tests required for licensure in the U.S. I'd attempted them early in my career and failed—miserably and repeatedly. The shame and disappointment were so crushing that I chose to focus on my career instead. I already felt behind. Hours at work were long. And with the sudden death of my father back home in Japan, I pushed that dream aside.

But that dream didn't disappear. It lingered like background noise I'd try to turn off. It hit me: I hadn't just let go of a goal. I had made its failure mean something about who I was.

Then—almost like the universe was nudging me—I stumbled on a podcast about life coaching. I didn't know it at the time, but that was the beginning of a deeper kind of transformation. One that didn't just help me revisit an old dream—but begin healing how I related to myself.

COACHING WASN'T JUST A TOOL—IT WAS A LIFELINE

It started with a podcast.

If you've ever fallen down the rabbit hole of a life coaching podcast, you know how it goes. One episode becomes five, then ten. Before long, you're bingeing hundreds of them, wondering how this stranger seems to know exactly what's going on in your brain.

That's how I found coaching. Or maybe how coaching found me.

At first glance, it probably looked like I was just adding more to my plate. I enrolled in a coaching membership through The Life Coach School. I was still muscling through, keeping all the balls in the air. But something about it stuck. There was a noticeable energetic shift. I began thinking differently—on purpose—about my circumstances, generating emotions that helped me take action toward my dreams.

For the first time in years, I found the energy to return to the ARE exams I'd long avoided. I passed three of the six. I earned my first coaching certification. I was working full-time in architecture. Coaching clients on the side. Studying for exams. Trying to stay present in my personal life.

On paper, I was thriving. But inside? I was over-functioning—stretching myself thinner and thinner to prove I could handle it all. Like so many women, I didn't recognize it as burnout. I was still performing. Still checking boxes. Still achieving. It wasn't until I began deeper work with my next coach and current mentor, Molly, that everything started to shift.

REDEFINING WHAT SUCCESS MEANS

For the first time, I was asked questions I'd never truly considered:

What does your ideal life look like?

What kind of business would actually support that life?

What do you want—not just what do you need?

They sound simple. But if your self-worth has been tied to selflessness, productivity, and achievement, those questions can feel. . . uncomfortable. Even indulgent. I was so used to sacrificing my personal life for professional progress, I'd stopped questioning it. I'd accepted that cost as the price of ambition. But, slowly, I began to see: the more I ignored myself, the less sustainable any version of success could be. That realization made me question everything I believed about what success really meant.

What if the way you've been taught to define success is the very thing burning you out? You've been praised for productivity. Rewarded for endurance. Conditioned to believe that rest is laziness—and slowing down means falling behind.

Especially for high-achieving women, success has often meant proving your worth through output—at the cost of your well-being. But what if real success isn't about doing more, but doing what matters? What if it's not about chasing more milestones, but aligning with who you truly are—and who you're becoming?

PATTERNS I SAW IN MY CLIENTS

As I pursued advanced training—first in Motherhood & Family Life coaching, then in Master Coach certification—I found myself leading from a different place. A place that made room for both ambition and well-being, for achievement and wholeness—for the full, messy, beautiful spectrum of a life aligned

And as I grew in my own work, I began to recognize the same quiet ache I had once carried showing up in my clients, no matter their background.

Some were men. Some were aspiring architects, just like I had been, wrestling with repeated failures on the ARE exams. Others were midlife women in leadership roles, juggling intense careers, motherhood, caregiving, and a restlessness they couldn't quite name.

Their lives looked different on paper. But the patterns were the same. None of them came to me saying they were burned out. They were driven. Intelligent. Deeply committed. Often the ones others leaned on most. But inside? They were stretched thin. Silently questioning their direction. Wondering if they just needed better time management—or if it wasn't supposed to feel this hard, this joyless, this disconnected.

If any part of that sounds familiar, take a breath. It doesn't mean you're doing it wrong. It may simply mean you're ready for a different kind of success.

YOU DON'T NEED ANOTHER TIME HACK

When clients first come to me, they're often hoping for practical fixes—better systems, sharper tools, smarter strategies. By the time most clients reach me, they're hoping for quick wins. Something to fix the exhaustion.

But the truth is: you don't need another time hack.
What you need is a new relationship with yourself.

One of my long-term clients—a male CEO of a small business in New York—carried an enormous load: managing client expectations, leading a team, overseeing projects, and trying to be present in his personal life. In our early sessions, accessing his emotions felt nearly impossible. Like many men, he'd learned—explicitly or not—that feeling was uncomfortable. Maybe even unsafe. Over time, he surprised himself. He built the emotional resilience to face hard conversations without shutting down. He learned to self-regulate under pressure. He even became a fan of EFT tapping—a tool he now uses regularly to stay grounded in the daily chaos.

That growth didn't just support his well-being—it transformed how he led.

In my early work with ARE exam candidates, I saw a different form of burnout—one rooted in chronic pressure and performance anxiety. Fear was everywhere: fear of failing, of being judged, of letting people down. Many carried quiet shame from past setbacks—just like I had. That shame created distance not just from their goals, but from themselves. What helped them weren't study strategies. It was mindset work. Nervous system awareness. Learning to manage energy. Once they had those tools, they didn't just study better. They passed.

THE REAL ISSUE ISN'T TIME—IT'S ENERGY

Then there was the woman who came to me hoping to improve her time management. A talented midlife architect running her own firm, she was juggling client work, business development, raising a family, and caring for aging parents.

No wonder she felt behind—her days were stretched beyond capacity.

> ....
>
> ## Most of you don't have a time problem. You have an energy problem.
>
> ....

But as we dug deeper, it became clear this wasn't just about optimizing her schedule. Her struggle wasn't really with time—it was with identity. Her self-worth had become entangled with how she used her time. She found it hard to set boundaries, say no, or prioritize herself without guilt.

Together, we worked across multiple layers:

Cognitive tools to shift her beliefs and build emotional resilience.

Nervous system regulation through gentle movement, tapping, breathwork, and meditation.

Practical, compassionate strategies tailored to her season of life.

By the end of our work together, her life no longer felt like a frantic juggling act. It had become something more intentional. More aligned. More alive. What her transformation revealed is something I see over and over:

Most of you don't have a time problem. You have an energy problem.

Time is constant. Everyone gets the same 24 hours. But your capacity to show up in those hours? That's energy. Energy isn't fixed. It's shaped by how you think, feel, and care for yourself. It can be created or drained—moment by moment. That's why one email, one conversation, or one walk outside can shift everything.

That's not time management. That's energy in motion.

A NEW WAY TO MANAGE THE DAY

When you start thinking in terms of energy instead of time, everything changes. For example: skipping a network event to go for a walk. Or saying no to a new project-even when it feels hard. Or something else. That's what I began teaching my clients: stop asking, "How can I squeeze this in?" and start asking, "Do I actually have the capacity for this today?" I call it energy budgeting.

Just like you wouldn't spend money you don't have—at least not on purpose—you can learn to notice when you're overspending your energy. On tasks. On people. On commitments that leave you depleted.

When clients begin budgeting their energy the way they budget money, something shifts. They start seeing what drains them, what restores them, and where they're overextending with little return. They begin designing their days with intention instead of urgency. Slowly, their lives begin to reflect not just their values—but their vitality.

This is the heart behind a free resource I created: "The Energy Budget Starter Kit." It's a simple, practical way to start paying attention to where your energy is really going—what depletes you and what sustains you. You can grab your free copy at
https://midore.myflodesk.com/energy-budgeting.

Burnout doesn't care if you're a CEO, a working mom, or an ambitious architect. It shows up when you abandon yourself in pursuit of what's supposed to make you feel like you're "enough." Recovery begins when you stop muscling through—and start listening inward.

COACHING LEADERS WHO DIDN'T KNOW THEY NEEDED IT

Have you ever thought, *Coaching sounds great. . . but it's not really for me?*

Maybe you're already successful. You've built a strong career. You manage teams, meet goals, and get things done. You're the one people rely on. So. . . why would you need coaching?

That's what several leaders in a recent training program quietly wondered, too. As part of the company's investment in its people, each manager was paired with a coach for one-on-one support. It was an incredible, forward-thinking offering—but not everyone was convinced.

Some asked, *Did I do something wrong? Why does my boss want me to do this?*

There was uncertainty. Resistance. Even fear.

A few expressed frustration about taking time away from their "real work" for training. And honestly, I understood. These were people navigating tight deadlines, high expectations, and emotional loads. Slowing down to reflect didn't feel productive—it felt indulgent.

I realized I was facing a learning curve, too. I was used to working with clients who *chose* coaching. For me, coaching had become a way of life—even a necessity. But this was different. These were leaders who hadn't sought it out. Many had never been invited to explore their inner world at work. That's what made it so powerful.

One manager in particular showed up to our first session with arms crossed, polite but clearly skeptical. Coaching, she said, felt like "one more thing" on her already overloaded calendar. But over time, our conversations shifted. She began sharing not just her team's challenges, but her own fears, her values, her vision. By the end of our work together, she was leading with more clarity and compassion—not just for her team, but for herself.

When the space was offered—with no agenda but support— some of the most lasting transformations began.

ALIGNMENT IS THE FOUNDATION

That coaching experience reminded me of something easy to forget—especially in high-achieving environments:

Even the most competent professionals—the ones everyone else relies on—need space to pause. To feel. To realign.

Because alignment isn't a luxury. It isn't selfish. And it isn't just personal. It's professional.

Alignment is what allows you to lead with clarity, make better decisions, and show up with presence. It's what sustains you when pressure builds. It's what helps you lead others without losing yourself. And it's not a one-time adjustment. It's an ongoing practice. One that's foundational to human-centered leadership— and essential to long-term success.

YOU DON'T HAVE TO BURN OUT TO GROW

Here's what I know now, deep in my bones: You don't have to burn out to be successful. You don't have to abandon yourself to keep everything running. You don't have to earn your worth by doing it all. Real success—the kind that feels meaningful and sustainable— starts from the inside out.

It starts when you listen inward.
When you get curious about what's no longer working.
When you give yourself permission to want more—not more to do, but more of you in the life you're building.

So if something in this chapter stirred something in you—
If you've found yourself asking, *Is this really the life I want?*

Please hear this:

You're not broken.
You're not behind.
And you are most definitely not alone.

You may be standing at the edge of something new.
Not a breakdown.
But a beginning.

CHAPTER 13

Why I Make Grown Men Cry

Patti Britt Kohler

Master Life & Relationship Coach, Speaker, Entrepreneur

 pattibrittcoaching.com

 instagram.com/pattibrittcoaching

 linkedin.com/in/pattibrittkohler

Patti Britt Kohler is a master certified life and relationship coach specializing in guiding high-achieving men through transformational personal growth. With a focus on helping clients who feel overwhelmed by the pressures of their responsibilities, past regrets, and future uncertainties, Patti's passion is to help men unlock their greatest potential to impact their families, businesses, and communities.

Her signature Midlife Renovation Model delivers immediate and lasting results with practical strategies along with emotional intelligence skills. Clients learn to regain control, find peace, and reignite their passion and purpose without needing to dismantle their lives.

Patti brings a wealth of experience and empathy to her work, understanding the challenges of feeling stuck or powerless. Her practical approach makes logical sense while being efficient and effective at helping clients experience breakthroughs, making her a trusted guide for men seeking to increase their potential.

Patti is also the co-founder of Main Street Professionals with her husband, Mark J. Kohler, where she serves as the life and performance coach for business professionals around the country.

She adores traveling and working with her husband, as well as precious time with her family, consisting of three adult children, four bonus children, and their growing families.

> They have a superpower they don't know exists
> That is the secret to their success
> *Patti Britt Kohler*

L adies, this chapter isn't for you, except that I want you to think about the man in your life you care for who appears to be distant, frustrated, burned out, or stuck. It could be your husband, son, or your father. Whoever it is, I want to give you hope that sharing this chapter with them could change their life. There truly is a remedy for what troubles them, and you might be surprised by what it is.

Men, a woman who loves you likely gave you this chapter to read, and I suspect you're humoring her by reading this, hoping to quickly get through it and maybe pull out a couple of quotes or anecdotes to get her off your back. Maybe you're thinking the sooner you can get this over with, the sooner you can get back to your project, the game, or something else on your list.

I've worked with and around a lot of men whose stories you might recognize. I grew up in the timber industry in the '80s and '90s watching my dad, uncles, and all sorts of rough and rugged guys logging the forests, driving trucks, running a sawmill, and managing the machinery shops.

I ultimately bought that sawmill, about 20 years ago, with my former husband, and spent a lot of time with these tough and wonderful men who worked with their hands. They would occasionally tell me their life stories and the struggles they were going through. Little did I know then that I was learning to speak their language. I could see their deepest fears and frustrations. I learned how to listen and ask questions that would sometimes make them go quiet and stare off into the distance, or hide the sight of tears welling up in their eyes.

At the time, I didn't fully understand why my questions drew such responses. For women, it seemed natural to talk about and experience feelings. For men, it was like touching a hot stove. Instinctively, I'd pull back. But I also felt I was helping them tap into a superpower they didn't know they had.

Years later, I discovered I had also been uncovering a skill and passion I had to help these strong and caring men. I learned what made them tick and why they suffered.

If John Gray was correct in his book *Men Are from Mars, Women Are from Venus*, I was learning to speak Martian and didn't even know it.

Fast forward 20 years. . .

I was in an afternoon Zoom call with a new client. His name was Don. From his intake form, I learned he was in his late forties, a professional working in a small firm, a family man, with typical hobbies, nothing out of the ordinary. Yet I also noted that in the section where I ask "Why are you here?" he wrote one word:

"Frustrated."

The short response on the form wasn't new. When it comes to men, they aren't usually prolific about their feelings. I knew that. Expected it. I was ready for him.

Right away, I could tell he didn't want to be there. Don just looked uncomfortable, and a little frustrated, as he'd clearly indicated.

I suspected his wife pushed him to sign up for some "coaching" and I could tell he thought it was just "woo-hoo." They had already done marriage counseling, and it always seemed like he was doing something wrong and he was made to feel like the bad guy. I'm sure he figured this new "coaching" thing was another attempt of hers to fix him.

Don wasn't having it. At least, not yet.

So, I started out with a few questions to get to know him and his circumstances. He was cagey and short, with matter-of-fact answers. As he talked about his work, he said, "My direct report just doesn't see my potential."

Then I asked about his marriage. . .

"My wife is trying and I'm trying, but it doesn't seem to be working or going anywhere good at this point."

I was going to bring up his sex life, but reserved that for later. I assumed that was a factor. It usually is.

And then, when it came to discussing extended family, it seemed everything was piling up for Don and working against him.

"My parents' health has been declining; I've got to step up and figure out something there. . . and my teenagers. I feel like I should be there for them more, but my work is so demanding."

I was hearing a lot of "shoulds" and "have to's" and "nothing is working" statements.

What Don was feeling was very common, and I wanted to see if he was serious about making some changes. I put him on the spot and asked some pointed questions. . .

"Don, do you feel like you're enough?" Of course, he said no.

"Do you feel like you're in control?" He just rolled his eyes.

"Do you trust your decisions right now?" That one, he didn't want to answer.

He appreciated the direct approach, but I knew he was done talking. Most men don't like to feel vulnerable or like they're "not enough." He certainly didn't want to show that side to me, either. He's a man. His generation doesn't talk about these things.

I said gently, "I suspect you feel stuck. In almost every area of your life."

As he looked down, he mumbled, "Yes." He didn't want to admit it.

I then knew what he really felt. He didn't need to verbalize it. He wouldn't. With all these people depending on him—at home, at work, and his parents—there was pressure. With everyone thinking he should have it all together but him not trusting himself, he felt doubt. With all the people around him assuming he should have it all figured out, he felt inadequate. But how could they know how he felt? He wouldn't, couldn't, admit his feelings to anyone. Even to himself.

After a long pause, I said, *"I bet you feel pretty lonely."*

His eyes started to well up with tears.

I was only on the call with him for a half hour and Don *knew* that I spoke his language. He knew I understood him. Now it was time to give him the solution, the path, and it was right there in front of him, and he just couldn't see it.

We'll pick this up in a moment. . .

Men, what do you think Don was wanting me to do? You know this. Just *tell* him what to *do*. Tell him what to change in his life, and how. He wanted to "action" his way out of his feelings. Like most men, he thought, *If I don't like the situation? Change it. If I don't like the people I'm around? Change them. If trying to control and change the people and world around me doesn't work, then I'll bury myself in something else, anything, that makes me feel better.*

Find a little happiness somewhere—on a golf course, in the woods, in a bottle, with a pill, surfing channels, watching porn. . .

anything to numb the loneliness or the pain. The bottom line is that when life doesn't go my way, the only option is to tough it out.

Men, you are supposed to be the heroes. So many people need you and rely on you to be providers and protectors. You want to be the hero, but that pressure can also be debilitating. When you don't know how to cope with it.

But there is another solution, and it's simple.

Your dad was wrong. You don't need to keep changing your circumstances to be happy, and you don't need to suck it up in order to get through. Silence doesn't mean strength.

Here is the "mic drop:" Those feelings you don't dare share with anyone, the loneliness, inadequacy, fear, or shame—they're okay! They are perfectly normal and don't say anything about you or what you're capable of. Emotions are harmless. They may come and go, but you have way more power over them than you know.

> ●
>
> Silence doesn't mean strength.
>
> ●

Men, I've seen you in the factory. I've seen you in the boardroom, on the job site, and in the corner office. I've seen you running the business that's the lifeline to everyone relying on you.

It's tough. Women don't always know the pressure you're under. And frankly, many don't understand what you want. Unless you recognize and understand these things yourself, you can't expect others to know them. There are common patterns for coping with life's challenges that keep you stuck and frustrated that, once you see for yourself, you can begin to change.

There are three things men generally do when they have feelings they don't like:

1. **Suppress them** – push the feelings down deep, only to find them leaking out in ways they're ashamed of.

2. **React to them** – let those feelings control their behavior and believe there's nothing they can do about it.

3. **Avoid them** – escape and numb their feelings with any distraction or dopamine hit they can find, regardless of the cost.

Even if there are adverse effects, many feel the ends justify the means.

But there's another option. One that will set you free and is the secret superpower for success. I'm serious. I've coached and taught hundreds of professional men, and I've seen this light go on for them and change their whole perspective on life.

And so, my journey with Don continued with a question that rocked his world.

After he admitted he was lonely and stuck, or so he thought, he just wanted me to give him that magic answer to make his problems go away.

He looked at me with some skepticism and I could hear him thinking, *Don't get me to admit all of that and then give me some stupid reason why I shouldn't feel that way.*

But instead, I asked, "What is so bad about feeling lonely?"

He was visibly speechless.

After blinking a few times, he blustered, "What do you mean? Haven't you ever felt lonely? It sucks!"

I said, "Tell me. . . please describe what 'lonely' feels like. Where in your body do you notice it?"

This was *not* what he expected.

In fact, this is a normal response I get from men that think "bad" feelings are like kryptonite: debilitating, uncontrollable, and something to avoid altogether. Remember, if you don't like what you're feeling, simply change the circumstance, *never ever* feel the feeling. Escape it. Suppress it. Numb it.

Don had never had to describe this foreign object before. They don't have those on Mars. That's a Venus thing. . . or so he thought. But the reality is, emotions are everywhere on Mars. They just don't acknowledge them, let alone talk about them.

"Come on, try," I gently prompted.

Don did his best."I guess it's heavy, uhhh. . . I don't know."

I continued, "How does it *actually* feel? Try to notice what's happening in your body."

He then said, "I guess there could be a lump in my throat. A tightening in my chest. A pit in my stomach?"

> Feelings won't kill you and they don't make you weak.

It took some guidance, but, slowly, he was able to notice the very real sensations in his body. He'd never taken the time to fully observe a strong emotion before. Something elusive and subjective for him suddenly became quantifiable and objective.

I then asked one of the most important questions of all, "Did that feeling kill you?"

He smiled and said "No."

"Did it lessen a bit or pass, like after smacking your finger with a hammer?"

He nodded and gave me a smirk. He realized this approach to describing an emotion was novel. It surprised him and immediately seemed to give him more control as he began to uncover the truth: Feelings won't kill you and they don't make you weak.

Over the next few weeks, what unfolded for Don was not what he expected. But it was life-changing.

My husband (who was also skeptical of coaching when we first met) once said something that stuck with me. He told me that guys just want things to "make sense;" when it's logical, they can accept it more easily and move on.

Don was unraveling for the first time that emotions actually do make sense—where they come from and why they exist. He learned that emotions are simply vibrations passing through the body with physical sensations connected to them. While uncomfortable and even painful at times, feelings are actually harmless.

Maybe you, like Don, make them more significant or dramatic, giving them more airtime and power in your life than they deserve. But having an emotion can often be experienced like stubbing your toe. We all know that sensation: while intense, it doesn't last forever. You realize all you can do is breathe and let it pass, like a current. Emotions typically flow much the same way, when they're allowed to.

Don, like my other clients, was learning that emotions aren't to be feared or avoided. In fact, he realized the very thing he had thought was "kryptonite" his whole life was something quite benign. As we continued to pinpoint and allow the experience of a "taboo" emotion that he'd kept bottled up for years, at times, there would be tears—tears of release and relief.

Through this process, Don also began to identify his common ways of thinking that were the actual cause of his emotions. His whole life, he'd attributed his feelings to other people or the situations he was in. He had no idea how much power he was actually giving away to others.

It was like waking up to a new reality. Waking up and having superpowers he didn't know existed. No one had ever shown him the true cause and effect of his thinking, feeling, and behaviors. No one had ever taught him the most valuable life skill: allowing an emotion and then redirecting his mind. He felt like he'd been given a new lease on life.

Not only was Don back in the driver's seat of his emotional life, he felt he had much more freedom and choice when it came to his relationships, roles, and responsibilities. He had a renewed sense of confidence, resilience, and control over his life.

How is Don doing now?

He's on fire! His marriage is better. Sex is better. He has more quality time with his kids, even if it's not always the quantity he wants. He's able to release the guilt, shame, and pressure that previously weighed him down and affected how he showed up with his wife and kids.

He's caring for his parents with a sense of gratitude and honor, not obligation. He's excited at work—serving his clients at a higher level, increasing his income, and making concrete plans to launch his own practice. Things he didn't believe he had the capacity or courage to do before we met.

We still meet every other week for maintenance and accountability. You see, our minds constantly get cluttered with new messes, and it's easy to slip back into old habits of thinking, feeling, and behaving.

But the good news with Don that makes this work so fulfilling? His actual circumstances really haven't changed much.

It's like the main character in the movie *City Slickers*. You've all seen it. When Mitch (played by Billy Crystal) comes back from the cattle drive a new man, nothing in his life had changed—only him! His approach to life. His mindset. His emotional clarity. And his renewed sense of purpose and passion. Curly, the trail boss, helped him find his "one thing," his purpose.

You, too, can have that "one thing!" When your perspective changes, everything changes.

Feelings are here to stay, I hate to tell you. I know it seems like a paradox, but there is always going to be an equal mix of positive and negative. It's part of what makes us fully human and alive.

But when you know you can handle them all, that truly no emotion can kill you, then you have the confidence and courage you need to tackle any challenge. You can allow emotions to ride along while you remain in the driver's seat.

So, what is the real superpower that all my clients are surprised to learn?

You get to choose what you think and how you feel! Your circumstances do not control your feelings. . . and feelings will never have control over you again—with practice, of course.

What you decide to think about your life and how you choose to let feelings come and go is your true power. And true freedom.

Check out my website, https://www.pattibrittcoaching.com/, to learn more. It's just for you gentlemen. Let's start your journey together. It may take you places you've never dreamed.

A cool byproduct, by the way, is that learning how to direct this sequence in your mind and body will give you the power to better influence and lead other people—like a magician! You can almost read their minds by knowing this simple truth: We all do things to either *avoid* a feeling or *have* a certain feeling.

Your clients, your employees, and your loved ones are all trying to feel a certain way, too. Once you are able to articulate and create that for yourself, you can motivate, inspire, and connect with others.

Life coaching is not "woo-hoo." It's logic, neuroscience, biology, and physiology. Don quickly figured that out, and later told me that, in our first session, I rocked his world in a way that countless hours of therapy never even came close to touching.

Men, you have now been given a gift and get to decide what you're going to do with it. A woman that loves you, and probably still doesn't understand you and your needs, gave you this chapter to read. Please do something with it.

Conclusion

I hope you've loved this book as much as we loved writing it for you.

I hope you always remember the moments of light and truth you felt as you read the words here.

I hope you can feel how much you matter.

The words in this book are more than just a project or a moment in time, they are an invitation to say yes to yourself. Each of the authors, including myself, have made that choice to say yes to ourselves, and there is a powerful ripple effect in this act. Because of this choice, we are here writing to you. We are impacting our families, our friends, and our communities in a more powerful way.

When you say "yes" to yourself and commit to creating the best life you can, you become a powerful light for others.

If you felt called to hire one of the coaches in this book, say "*yes.*"

If you've felt called to become a coach yourself, say "*yes.*"

If you've felt called to do that thing, make that choice, or finally release what no longer serves you, say "*yes.*"

We are here with you, in solidarity, all 13 of us: you've got this, and we've got you.

XO,
Molly

Are You Interested in Becoming a Master Certified Coach?

The Masterful Coach Collective® is where committed coaches come to refine their skills, expand their impact, and achieve true mastery. Inside this training, you'll learn the *Four Fundamentals of Lasting Change* and gain the tools to guide clients through profound transformation in life, business, and relationships. If the work in this book resonates with you, I'd be honored to mentor you on the path to mastery.

To learn more visit:
https://www.mollyclaire.com/master-coach-training

Will You Share the Love?

If you've enjoyed *She Rises*, the authors have a favor to ask.

Would you consider giving it a rating wherever you bought the book? Online book stores are more likely to promote a book when they feel good about its content, and reader reviews are a great barometer for a book's quality.

Also, if you have found this book valuable and know others who would find it useful, consider buying them a copy as a gift. Special bulk discounts are available if you would like your whole team or organization to benefit from reading this. Just contact team@ mollyclaire.com.